A Professional's Guide to Promoting Self-Discovery in Youth

A Creative-Based Curriculum

I am an ARTIST creating my life NOW!

This book belongs to:

_____

Contact information if found:

_____

"That which we are, we shall teach."
RALPH WALDO EMERSON

A Professional's Guide
to Promoting
Self-Discovery in Youth

A Creative-Based Curriculum

By

Lissa Masters, Ph.D., ATR

CHARLES C THOMAS • PUBLISHER, LTD.
Springfield • Illinois • U.S.A.

Published and Distributed Throughout the World by

CHARLES C THOMAS • PUBLISHER, LTD.
2600 South First Street
Springfield, Illinois 62704

© 2017 by CHARLES C THOMAS • PUBLISHER, LTD.

ISBN 978-0-398-09184-2 (paper)
ISBN 978-0-398-09185-9 (ebook)

With THOMAS BOOKS *careful attention is given to all details of manufacturing
and design. It is the Publisher's desire to present books that are satisfactory as to their
physical qualities and artistic possibilities and appropriate for their particular use.*
THOMAS BOOKS *will be true to those laws of quality that assure a good name
and good will.*

Printed in the United States of America
LM-C-1

Library of Congress Cataloging-in-Publication Data

Names: Masters, Lissa, author.
Title: A professional's guide to promoting self-discovery in youth : a
    creative-based curriculum / by Lissa Masters, Ph.D., ATR.
Description: Springfield, Illinois, U.S.A. : Charles C Thomas, Publisher,
    LTD, [2017] | Includes bibliographical references and index.
Identifiers: LCCN 2017020484 (print) | LCCN 2017025757 (ebook) | ISBN
    9780398091859 (ebook) | ISBN 9780398091842 (paper)
Subjects: LCSH: Creative thinking--Study and teaching. | Creative teaching.
    | Arts--Study and teaching. | Holistic education. | Self-culture.
Classification: LCC LB1590.5 (ebook) | LCC LB1590.5 .M28 2017 (print)
    | DDC 370.15/7--dc23
LC record available at https://lccn.loc.gov/2017020484

FOR THE CHILDREN:
Those who are grown,
those who are growing,
and those who have not yet arrived.

Preface

It is with the proper alignment of the stars that this book has manifested. The words waited patiently, and have now jumped excitedly onto these pages to form a tool that can serve in revolutionizing education. Education is the alchemical key to the evolution and enlightenment of humanity. This curriculum (Lessons for Living Program™) is especially intended for art therapists, therapists, life coaches, and counselors to bring into school environments with adopted holistic principles. Its contents offer youth a foundational program of self-exploration, an important support for all other learning that will take place in preparation for adulthood. I am honored to be a part of this book's mission, and I extend gratitude to everyone who played a role in its production.

— Lissa Masters

Acknowledgments

**I would like to express my deep appreciation to the following people
who have been influential in paving the way for this book.**

My children Daniel and Lara, whose loving presence and support continually makes my heart sing. The students and colleagues at Briggs High School and Norwalk High School in Connecticut, who over many years motivated me to tap into a wellspring of inner resources and led me to the doorway of art therapy. Also, heart-filled acknowledgements to the "family" at Rising Star Montessori School in Alameda, California. I am grateful for the many students that I have had the opportunity to "create" with along the way—your smiles and laughter are with me always.

Sincere gratitude also to:
Joseph Mola for professional guidance and support during my public school teaching career.
Ann Gavey, Rex Higgenbotham, and Katrina Ross
for welcoming me to the Montessori philosophy.

Contemporary holistic educators: There are many...especially
Sonnie McFarland, John Miller, Ron Miller, Jerry Mintz, Parker Palmer
for your inspiring work in education for a new world.
Shaun McNiff and Natalie Rogers
for your soulful, pioneering contributions to the field of art therapy
and person-centered expressive arts therapy.
... And other outstanding art therapy professionals who I have encountered on my path.

AND:
Mark Weiman and Regent Press for editing expertise, technological assistance,
and unwavering encouragement.
Alan Rinzler for assisting writers to become respected authors.
Warwick Associates for exceptional book consulting expertise.
Beth Barany for valuable book coaching skills.
Claire Rose for manuscript feedback, and trust in this project's unfoldment.
Sandy Billings for excellent insight and suggestions.
Hooriyeh Biganpour for graphic arts assistance.
Trevor Ollech, Craig Coss, Kelly Alterman for artistic vision and computer graphic skills.
Dorothea Joyce for your creative inspiration in the early stages of this project.
Barbara Dandridge for computer mentoring.
Rich and Yoko Clark for moral support, and providing me a perfect workspace.
My feline friends: Loa, Kea, & Zia for your loving companionship, especially beside the computer.
The following organizations: A.A.T.A., A.E.R.O., A.M.A., I.E.A.T.A., I.M.M.

ALSO:
Gratitude to my parents Barbara and Durland Stewart, family,
extended family and friends for your love. Big hugs to Julie, Louisa & Ayla.
A special thank you to a divine support team: Gabriel, Michael, Allisone, and inspiring holistic pioneers who have left their legacy here, especially Maria Montessori.
And, thank YOU facilitators who are taking the reins and all the students who will say "yes" to becoming skilled artists in the ART of Life. Your work and service benefits us all!

Namaste

Table of Contents

A Professional's Guide
to Promoting
Self-Discovery in Youth

A Creative-Based Curriculum

Introduction

The ideas that formulated this book began to percolate in the early nineties. I had been hired for an art teacher position at a small, public alternative high school in Norwalk, Connecticut; a place where the city sequestered potential "dropouts," and faculty shepherded them toward a graduating diploma. The school accommodated pregnant teens and their preschoolers, the smaller student/teacher ratio benefited students with behavior issues, and the school's early dismissal helped to curb habitual delinquency.

In the earlier days the school offered vocational training along with core subjects required for graduation. Students could focus on automotive repair, metal shop, typing, or cooking, giving students additional assurance for entering the workforce. The art room at this time served as a popular haven where students could relax, socialize, and learn new art skills. Most importantly, it became a space where opportunities were provided to express strong emotions through art-making.

Each morning students lumbered into my classroom appearing lethargic and defeated, sometimes excited, or perhaps angry and agitated. It was important to be skillfully attentive to each individual's needs. Many students carried troubling stories they wanted to share, and confronted decisions that were difficult to navigate. I found myself naturally using art experiences to assist students in understanding their feelings. Artwork became a vehicle of communication and a tool for emotional healing. Exhibiting their creations in the school hall enhanced the student's self-esteem, and although there was an ongoing concern with vandalism, this art was only admired. Some art was just about the process. These pieces were hidden or discarded after the student witnessed revealing aspects. However, these too contributed toward the emergence of a healthy sense of self.

It was soon apparent why my art room seemed to magnetize students. One afternoon after I described my day's activities, a colleague explained how I was providing a kind of "art therapy," a term I was not familiar with at the time. I was very interested in learning more about how therapeutic art activities could be used in a classroom. Fellow art teachers suggested I read Peter London's book, *No More Secondhand Art*. His words spoke to me so deeply that I eagerly enrolled in a weeklong summer intensive that he taught in Massachusetts. I supported London's recognition of how art can be considered a sacred artifact. He compared this to ancient primal people making art not merely for decoration or self-expression, but rather a vehicle of profound personal or collective transformation. That summer class proved to be a "peak" experience that nudged me to change my career intentions, as I later pursued graduate work in art therapy at Pratt Institute in New York. The diagnostic and analysis theories that I learned were interesting, but what really excited me were the experiential benefits of art for self-discovery and attaining "wholeness."

I was still teaching at the school as I continued my studies, steadily introducing my students to new activities each year that were intrinsically motivating. The curriculum I developed was well-rounded. It consisted of a basic art foundation with an exploration of various media, and included exercises practiced individually or in small groups to promote personal discovery. It became evident that the emotional needs of my students were being addressed more fully through art-making. To broaden the experience I provided exercises on basic life skills that I felt were neglected, yet vital. These art activities examined the physical, mental, emotional, and spiritual components of the individual. I was drawn to the work of pioneer art therapist, Shaun McNiff, who spoke of art being akin to "soul medicine." McNiff's philosophy of art and its therapeutic value strongly inspired my personal ideology. My own "toolbox" was forming, already filled with a spiritual intention that I believed was all encompassing; and with this, tools gathered from wise teachers who met me on my path.

In 1998 life presented me with a huge "Yield" sign, as I suddenly was thrust into a serious health challenge. My recovery was an opportunity to learn more about the healing arts, and find more balance in my life by taking better care of my own needs. I was fascinated by Judith Cornell's work about mandalas, Lucia Capacchione's work with journaling, and Carolyn Myss's work that centered on the intuitive energetic body we all possess. It was time to change my lifestyle, and what a better place to do that in but California. I left my job and headed there in 2001, feeling renewed and liberated.

Northern California was idyllic for almost four years. I concentrated on expressing all the art forms that hungered for my personal attention. Music, chanting, writing, theatre, abstract painting, and Barbara Mettler style dancing were areas I happily immersed myself in, supported by newfound friends and holistic living. In 2004, I moved back to the East Coast to be closer to family. There on the outer banks of North Carolina I met a woman at a drumming circle who described herself as an expressive arts therapist. I was intrigued, because my own therapeutic "toolbox" was now heavy with a plethora of expressive art modalities.

This encounter led me to the doorsteps of Appalachian State University where I was introduced to Sally Atkins, a highly regarded expressive arts therapy instructor whom I studied with briefly.

Life on the East Coast felt unsettling, and in 2005 I returned "home" to California. Once again regaining balance, I explored the array of options available for the schooling of children—still a primary passion. I read many books about non-traditional approaches to learning. I applied to work at a Montessori school in the Bay area after feeling ignited by Maria Montessori's writings in her numerous books. Her regard for honoring the natural physical, mental, emotional, and spiritual development of every child resonated with me.

In 2008 my dedication to improve our education system propelled me into a postgraduate study of holistic counseling. I began to write a curriculum that could be used in progressive learning environments. My experience at the Montessori school helped me to shape the format for this endeavor. Of course, the curriculum would need to weave creativity with a structure of life lessons that would guide students to make positive, conscious choices. The work of Natalie Rogers and her person-centered approach to expressive arts therapy was influential to my book's content. I was first introduced to this philosophy in 2010, when I attended a series of expressive arts workshops with therapists Anin Utigaard and Sophia Reinders who shared how they apply this work in clinical practice. Roger's encouragement of counselors to "follow a client," and ways to creatively connect a combination of art processes to promote well-being, aligned with my intentions. I began a certificate program with Natalie Rogers in 2013 to further integrate her work with my contribution to art therapy and education.

The knowledge garnered on my path culminated in this facilitator guide, which offers a means for self-awareness and discovery. The curriculum begins with an exploration of the Physical Body, followed by the Mental, Emotional, and Spiritual Body. Each domain has ten lessons, each one initially presented by the facilitator. Students use self-inquiry to explore a lesson as far as they choose, creative expressive activities help answer their questions. Parents and teachers have appreciated this meaningful holistic curriculum (Lessons for Living Program™) that ensures a more complete educational experience for children. This learning affords students an ability to mark their journey from child to adulthood with ease and confidence. Children enjoy participating in the engaging lessons, and relish the personal insight gained from them. So too, the program instills in students a significant respect for all people and life forms—a generous gift that radiates peace for our planet.

It is my hope that facilitators will find the exercises in this book useful in a variety of settings, and as a result be instrumental in bringing forth the potential of many lives.

Dear Earth Student,

The education you will receive costs nothing but takes a lifetime in order to graduate. Upon completion you may choose to further advance your learning, taking another lifetime to meet all requirements. You may then choose yet again another area of study, and on, and on, and on. In other words, this curriculum never ends, as the syllabus is constantly being revised. It is, however, highly recommended, and I am always available for help.

P.S. You are already enrolled. It's called Life.

Love,
Your Creator

NOTES for FACILITATORS

This curriculum is especially for:

- *All students in grades four, seven, and ten.* (The curriculum lessons can be repeated at different stages of a student's growth toward maturity—allowing for new self-discoveries to be made and to reinforce the learning concepts.) A two-and-a-half-month study in each domain is the suggested timeframe for a typical ten-month school year.

It also can be of interest to:

Professional teaching staff/parents who have this curriculum implemented at their school—to become familiar with its content, or *Other adults* as a tool for self development.

Student Supply List

It is suggested that all student materials be marked with names and stored together for safekeeping. Students may take home any of their materials at the completion of the curriculum.

1. Journal (lined or unlined)
2. 18" x 24" wallet art portfolio (paper or cardboard)
3. 1 $\frac{1}{2}$" three-ring binder
4. Package of plastic page protectors for binder (optional)

FACILITATOR MATERIALS

An ideal room for this program is large enough for students to move around in, and sit together on a rug for presentations. Large tables for art-making are preferred.

Facilitator Guide

Personal files for notes, samples, ideas

Resource books

Computer with Internet access

Library resources

Copy machine availability

Laminating machine availability (Color-copy personal photos before laminating.)

Camera

Tables, chairs

Table coverings or newspaper

Floor pillows (optional)

Sink access

Bucket

Sponges

Soap

Paper towels/rags

Display easel

Paper cutter

Three hole punch

Disposable gloves

Smock

Talking stick (optional) (Embellish a small branch with a feather, beads, etc.)

White votive candles and holder, matches

Earth globe

Plastic containers for storing art supplies and prepared lesson materials

Art portfolio for flat display materials

Technological materials: The use of technology may be preferred by some facilitators. Facilitators who have access to these materials can incorporate them as they see fit.

GENERAL ART SUPPLIES

White board

Dry erase markers

White drawing paper (12" x 18")—can be cut to size as needed

Watercolor paper (11" x 14")

White poster board

White copy paper or recycled paper (to fit in binder inserts—8 1/2" x 11")

White or beige mural paper

White heavyweight paper (18" x 24")—can be cut to size as needed

Construction paper (assorted colors)

Tissue paper (assorted colors)

Canvas board panels (about 11" x 14" for individuals, 18" x 24" for group project)

Thin cardboard (11" x 14")

Medium-weight cardboard (11" x 14")

Assortment of colored pencils

Assortment of colored felt-tip markers (wide and thin)

Black permanent markers (wide or thin)

Assortment of crayons

Baskets for distributing drawing supplies

Plastic containers with lids for mixed paints in mural-making

Water containers for painting

Plastic pitcher for pouring water

Egg cartons for students to mix paints

Watercolor sets

Tempera paints (at least the basics of: red, yellow, blue, black, white)—I like to have an assortment of other colors in smaller sizes.

Acrylic paints (at least the basics of: red, yellow, blue, black, white, gold)—These are more economical and easier to handle in plastic bottles than tubes.

Assortment of brushes for acrylic and water-based paints—Younger children work best with short handles.

Gesso primer

Smocks

Pencils

Pencil sharpeners

Erasers

Rulers

Scissors

X-acto knife

Transparent tape

Masking tape

White glue

Glue sticks

Hot glue guns

Hot glue sticks

Non-hardening modeling clay

Assorted rubber stamps

Stamp pads

Glitter

Collage Material—Many things can be saved or acquired for collage.

Magazines (a large selection of these that are age appropriate for the group)

Nature finds: leaves, seeds, feathers, shells, twigs, bark, pebbles . . .

used greeting cards	*embroidery thread*	*old calendars*
small fabric scraps	*craft odds & ends*	*broken jewelry*
party paper scraps	*corks*	*felt scraps*
yarn	*buttons*	*pom-poms*
sequins	*ribbon*	*stickers*

Note: Other specific materials may be needed for CREATIVE ACTIVITIES.

These are the suggested basic materials. Feel free at your discretion to offer other media for drawing activities. I like to stay away from chalk and oil pastels—both require spray fixative and tend to be messy. Look into acquiring free donations of paper from print shops; or check recycle depots for inexpensive art supplies.

GENERAL GUIDELINES for FACILITATORS

- Be enthusiastic. Providing an informational meeting with parents to introduce the curriculum (Lessons for Living Progam™), is appropriate for most student groups.
- Bless the journey and all that will unfold.
- Permit groups to bond initially through group introductions and warm-up games.
- Encourage students to sit in a circle on a rug for presentations. A large group of students may be divided into smaller groups for creative activities.
- Follow the sequence of the curriculum as the experiences build on each other and follow like a roadmap for self-discovery. Use your discretion in modifying general lesson contents to adapt for different age levels.
- Adhere to general and ethical guidelines for group process (e.g., confidentiality, "I" statements, non-judgment, respect for others, right to pass). Share guidelines with students.
- Establish timeframe for expressive art explorations depending on the needs of the group and the specific activity.
- Be present with students during all phases of the creative exercises. Offer personal support to any student exploring deep, fragile issues.
- Give students time to acquaint themselves with their artwork and writing processes.
- Encourage group sharing. Emphasize active listening—with positive regard, empathy, and non-judgement. Direct participant's dialogue about other students' artwork to: expressing personal feelings, a clarifying inquiry, or to note symbology such as in archetypes.
- Incorporate other expressive art modalities that could enhance the journey in each particular group dynamic.
- Use a camera to photograph group process or artwork. Collect personal notes. (Permission to photograph artwork or students may be required.)
- Allow time for students to assist in clean up.
- Include a ritual of closure and gratitude after each meeting.
- Allocate sign-up time for students to meet with you for personal counseling or "check-in" during the course of the program.

CURRICULUM GUIDELINES

1. Begin the exploration of each domain by first creating an environment that reflects the theme to spark student curiosity. If possible, decorate the room with related visuals and books.

2. Prepare and gather materials for sub-heading lessons. (Copy Lesson Cover/ SI pages & MK/NTM pages double-sided—see templates g-j. — Instead of copying PAGES for writing lesson information you may choose to just use journals.)

3. Introduce each new domain by sharing some general facts.

4. Begin each sub-heading topic with the main lesson Presentation. (**Simplify basic information and discussion for younger students.**)

5. Provide students with a blank copy of the <u>Lesson Cover/SELF-INQUIRY PAGE</u>, and allow time for each student to come up with their own questions (see Author pages). (**Younger children may fill out only a few responses for written pages.**)

6. Present CREATIVE ACTIVITIES during the course of a week, or own time frame. (**Select the activities that you feel comfortable with and are best suited for your group.**)

7. Provide students with a blank copy of <u>MY KNOWLEDGE PAGE/NOTES TO MYSELF</u> to fill out as they work through the creative processes (see Author pages). Encourage the use of book and Internet sources for research.

8. Facilitate group or partner sharing for each lesson where applicable. Emphasize good communication and listening skills.

9. Large artwork can be saved in portfolios; other artwork, written exercises, and photocopies can be put into student binders.

10. Clean up.

11. End meetings with a closing ritual.

12. Co-create a ceremony after completing the entire program. Celebrate each student's journey with *Student Certificate of Participation.*

Note: The Author pages have been included to provide additional information for the facilitators, and are the result of the author's personal journey through the lessons. Facilitators can use this information however they choose.

Creative expression in its higher form reflects the true nature of our being.

MESSAGE to PARENTS

Lessons for Living Program™

We are all a part of a creative matrix that originates from love. It is the energy of which we have come and that to which we will eventually return. We can choose to significantly emanate this love in our lives now by moving to a higher expression of our being. The question that arises then is this: How are we allowing our creative energy to be used? We create our lives with every thought and choice. We can learn to make choices from an awareness of what best serves us, and the greater good of others.

The Lessons for Living Program™ is based on forty lessons that guide students through an exploration of the four domains of the self: physical, mental, emotional, and spiritual. Each lesson provides expressive art activities to enhance the process and to generate meaningful content. It is by knowing ourselves first that anything in life makes sense or has purpose. The discoveries made from this journey empower students as the artists of their own lives in creating a masterpiece.

Professional Program Facilitator: _____

Child's Name: _____

Yes, I give _____ permission to participate in this program.

Parent/Guardian Signature _____

This program is based on the book, *A Professional's Guide to Promoting Self-Discovery in Youth: A Creative-Based Curriculum* by Lissa Masters, Ph.D., ATR.

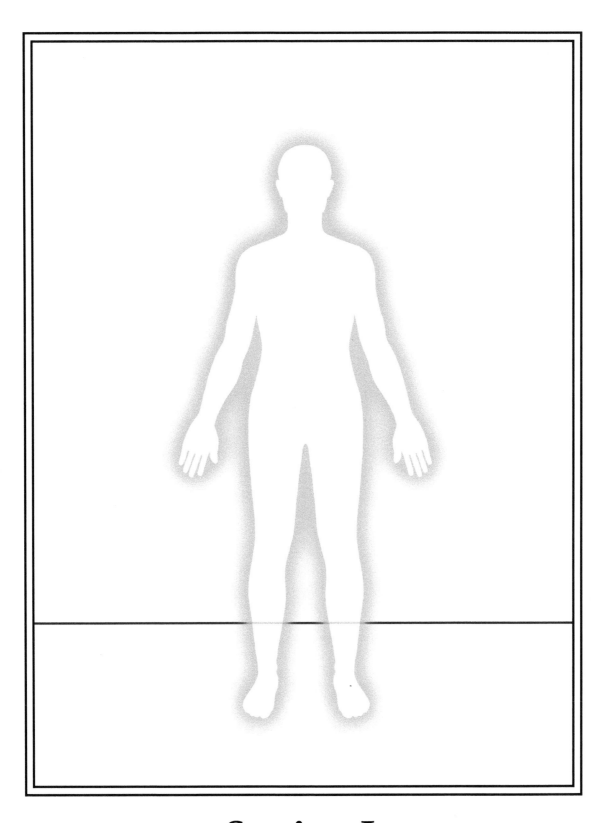

Section I:
The PHYSICAL SELF

The
PHYSICAL
SELF

ENERGY/The Physical Body/ CREATIVITY

Our physical self is an energy system made up of the same light particles as the stars. The physical body is our vehicle for life on this planet. Let's explore the Physical Self and its related aspects through the creative process.

Here are some FACTS about our PHYSICAL SELF:

- The heart beats about 100,000 times a day.
- The adult human body is comprised of 206 bones; 106 are in the hands and feet.
- A baby grows to about three times its birth weight by the first year.
- The human begins as a single cell and develops into a body consisting of trillions of cells.
- Our skin, as the largest organ, protects inner organs and keeps our body at the proper temperature.
- DNA is arranged in a double helix and resides within all living things.
- The ears and nose continue to grow throughout one's life.
- It takes about twelve hours for our body to completely digest food.
- Fingerprints are unique, as well as our tongue prints.
- Our physical energy communicates to others before words are spoken.

The Physical Self

1. Body
2. Nutrition
3. Exercise
4. Rhythm
5. Energy Centers
6. Sexuality
7. Senses
8. Bodywork
9. Environment
10. Breath

1. Body

Preparation

> Collect an assortment of popular body care products for discussion (e.g., shampoo, soap, body lotion, toothpaste, deodorant, mouthwash).

> Obtain an information sheet listing unsafe ingredients found in body care products (Internet source). Make a copy for each student.

Materials

Human internal body illustration (Internet source) or model, body care products, information sheets, magnifying glass, organic hand lotion

Presentation

INTRODUCTION—Invite students to explore the Body, an aspect related to our PHYSICAL SELF. Ask students what they know or think they know about the Body.

a. Discuss the ways in which we can become more tolerant and appreciative of body diversity. Our human body is a vehicle for this life—unique in shape, size, and physical characteristics.

b. Explain how we can choose to respect and take care of our bodies with proper diet, exercise, and attention to wellness habits. Regular physical and dental check-ups help maintain optimal health.

c. Show the internal human body illustration. The physical body's internal structure is directly related to our mental, emotional, and spiritual bodies.

d. Discuss good grooming habits. Grooming needs change as our bodies grow and mature.

e. Discuss the ways we take care of our body using health and beauty products.

f. Display body care products. Ask students which products they have heard about through advertising media. Explain why it is best to purchase natural, fragrance-free products. Natural body care products do not include preservatives that cause skin irritations; fragrance-free products do not include perfumes that can have the same result. (The cosmetic industry often uses the word "natural," even though synthetic/toxic ingredients may have been used in manufacturing.)

g. Read and look up information together about the ingredients on each collected product label. (Use the magnifying glass for small print.) Determine which products are made using the most natural ingredients. Look to see which contain ingredients that raise health concerns (e.g., Sodium Laurel Sulfate (SLS), a common detergent used in shampoo has been linked (based on scientific research) to causing eye damage in young children, skin damage, cancer, and premature baldness).

h. Discuss the importance of making educated decisions when selecting personal care products. Consumers need to check ingredients on body care products to avoid harmful effects. (The FDA encourages companies to collect information about dangerous ingredients on the market and to warn consumers, yet this is not compulsory. The FDA, however, is obligated to make its findings public.)

i. Give each student a dollop of the lotion to massage hands.

CLOSING—Ask students to comment. What questions do they have about the Body? Questions can be written on their SELF-INQUIRY PAGE for exploration and research.

Name __Author__

Section __Physical__   Lesson __1 – Body__

SELF-INQUIRY PAGE

What questions do I want to ask my doctor at my next yearly physical?

Are the ingredients in my body care products safe and non-toxic?

What changes can I make to optimize my appearance?

Do I need to use sunblock daily?

What items from my wardrobe am I ready to give away?

1. Body

CREATIVE ACTIVITIES

1. Make a list of all of your personal care products. Look at your product labels and research information about any ingredients you are not familiar with. Rate the products from 1 to 5, with 5 being the most natural. Discard products with potentially harmful chemical ingredients. What replacements can you make that are chemical-free? (Materials: paper, pencil)

2. Design an appreciation award for your hands. They work long hours for you every day. Trace your hands on paper and decorate an award for their services. What special treatment might they appreciate now? (Materials: paper, pencil, rubber stamps, stamp pads, colored pencils, markers, white glue, glitter)

3. Take an inventory of your closet and gather clothes and accessories you are ready to donate. Organize a clothing swap with your group. In what ways can any clothes be altered to create a new fashion statement? How often do you wear clothes that are made from natural fibers? Educate yourself on clothing companies that practice ethical manufacturing. (Materials: recyclable clothes)

4. Respect yourself and others as a "work of art." Divide your group with half being "sculptures," the other half visitors to the "museum." The "sculptures" will need to maintain a comfortable pose for about five minutes. They are lovingly viewed not as friends, but as unique art forms. Roles are then reversed. How did each role feel? (Materials: none)

5. Find out how to make your own natural body care product (e.g., soap, shampoo, hand cream, facemask). Is the scent appealing? Design your own fancy label. (Materials: materials as needed)

Body –cont.

Sample illustration by the Author: Activity 2.

Additional Ideas for Exploration

- Get a medical check-up and gather wellness information for your body's age and condition.
- Discover and explore recommendations for your ayurvedic (an ancient holistic wellness approach from India) body type (dosha) = Vata, Pitta, or Kapha.
- Read about the varied uses of essential oils (concentrated elements extracted from parts of plants).
- Invent a new hairstyle for yourself or a friend.
- Learn how to give yourself a manicure and/or pedicure. Polish and decorate your nails (or a friends).

Name ___Author___

Section ___Physical___ Lesson 1 – Body

MY KNOWLEDGE PAGE
(INFORMATION, DISCOVERIES, AND QUESTIONS)

Healthy gums and mouth have a positive effect on heart health.

I can help to prevent skin problems resulting from exposure to the sun's rays by wearing protective clothing, and using sunblock. I will look for a natural mineral-based sunblock (containing zinc oxide). A mineral-based sunblock sits on the surface of the skin unlike many chemical-based sunscreens.

What fragrances in body care products do I prefer?

My thoughts and feelings contribute to the wellness of my physical body.

Evidence supports the idea that the body moves through seven-year cycles of change. This cycle affects the physical body by cell change; and the mental, emotional, spiritual bodies by shifts in attitude and lifestyle.

Name ___Author___

Section ___Physical___ Lesson ___1 – Body___

NOTES TO MYSELF

Make a dental appointment!

Polyester fabrics aggravate my skin.

Try a new hairstyle.

Give my hands and feet regular massages.

Update my wardrobe.

FACILITATOR NOTES

2. Nutrition

Preparation

> Make a Healthy Eating Plate. Use tape to divide a plate into food sections (see template). Label sections as shown.

> Make Food Picture cards. Find magazine/Internet images (or draw your own) for each category of the Healthy Eating Plate. Cut out or glue onto white paper for about thirty cards. Laminate for repeated use.

> Prepare healthy food samples. Cut up an assortment of organic fruits and/or vegetables and arrange them on a plate.

Materials

Healthy Eating Plate, Food Picture cards, healthy food samples

Presentation

INTRODUCTION—Invite students to explore Nutrition, an aspect related to our PHYSICAL SELF. Ask students what they know or think they know about Nutrition.

a. Discuss good nutrition and why our bodies require healthy foods and clean water to function optimally. The expression, "You are what you eat," means that whatever you eat affects the health of the entire body. It is important that our bodies are given foods that contain valuable nutrients to build organs and tissues; and for the fuel we need to grow, learn, and play. Addictions to sugar, alcohol, drugs, and "junk" food may require the help of a professional counselor to overcome.

b. Display Healthy Eating Plate. Explain the requirements for a balanced diet. (A balanced diet can promote health, prevent disease, and maintain a healthy weight.) Consider eating a variety of foods from the different food groups each day–emphasizing vegetables, fruits, and whole grains.

c. Discuss the healthy foods that comprise each section.
   1. <u>Vegetables</u> (varied & colorful—limit potatoes).
   2. <u>Fruits</u> (varied & colorful).
   3. <u>Whole Grains</u> (whole graim bread, pasta, brown rice—limit refined grains).
   4. <u>Healthy Protein</u> (fish, poultry, beans, nuts—limit red meat, cheese). Also, as part of this healthy diet include Healthy Fats/Oils—(olive,

canola—limit butter); Water, tea/coffee—limit milk/dairy/ juice.

d. Present Food Picture cards. Have students place the cards in the appropriate sections on the plate.

e. Determine what foods should be consumed only occasionally (e.g., fast food, sugar-sweetened beverages, unhealthy fats, food products with sugar as one of the first three ingredients).

f. Explain the food terms: natural, organic, and certified organic. *Natural* foods are comprised of ingredients that are derived from nature. *Organic* foods are the result of a sustainable system of farming that produces healthy plants. *Certified organic* is a claim from a third party that the final product is guaranteed to derive from organic practices and methods. (Farmers' markets are a fun way to shop for a variety of organic food; volunteering at a community garden offers the reward of harvesting free fresh produce.)

g. Explore the principles of specific diets (e.g., vegetarian, vegan, raw food, gluten-free, ayurvedic, macrobiotic). Discuss the healthier methods for cooking—such as steaming vegetables versus frying.

h. Discuss the importance of cleaning hands properly before handling food. Also, washing fruits and vegetables before eating or meal preparation.

i. Discuss the benefits of eating regular moderate meals and chewing food well to aid digestion.

j. Share healthy food samples with students.

CLOSING—Ask students to comment. What questions do they have about Nutrition? Questions can be written on their SELF-INQUIRY PAGE for exploration and research.

Name __Author__

Section __Physical__   Lesson __2 – Nutrition__

SELF-INQUIRY PAGE

How do different vibrations of food affect me?

Are there any vitamin supplements that would benefit me at this time?

How can I test the quality of my drinking water?

Am I allergic to any foods?

What is the best diet for my body now?

2. Nutrition

CREATIVE ACTIVITIES

1. Make a list of foods you eat regularly for breakfast, lunch, dinner, and snacks in-between. Include beverages. How healthy is your present diet? Do you over-consume sugar or caffeine? Study a chart on acidic/alkaline foods (Internet source). Do you eat enough alkalizing foods to keep your acid/alkaline levels balanced? (Materials: paper, pencil, food chart)

2. Consider the energy frequencies of various food samples (e.g., certified organic produce, non-organic produce, a processed food, a piece of candy). Include samples of favorite snacks and beverages, as well as drinking water from different sources. What foods do you "feel" have a higher vibration? The "purest" foods will carry the highest energy, and be most nutritious. What are the ingredients in lower vibrating foods? (Materials: food samples)

3. Use a Body Outline (see template) and write the foods from your food list (Activity 1.) inside. Indicate the healthiest foods near the top, and lower vibrating foods in the bottom half of the outline. What new food choices can you make for good nutrition? Do you drink enough water throughout the day? (Materials: Body Outline copy, colored pencils)

4. Prepare a high-energy organic salad to share with friends. Choose a rainbow of colorful cut-up vegetables with mixed green lettuce. How do you feel after eating this meal? (Materials: organic lettuce, organic salad vegetables, strainer, cutting board, vegetable peeler, knife, salad bowl, tongs, organic dressing, plates and forks for serving)

5. Visit a health food store and explore healthy nutrition options. Familiarize yourself with product ingredients. What are good choices for some common grocery items? Snacks? Beverages? Share what you have learned with family members to help select healthy grocery items when shopping at your favorite store. (Materials: paper, pencil)

Nutrition –cont.

Sample illustration by the Author: Activity 3.

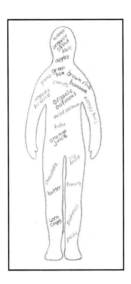

Additional Ideas for Exploration
- Plan a nutritious potluck party with your group. Write down recipes to share.
- Follow a recipe to make a healthy fruit smoothie/shake.
- Visit an organic garden or farmers' market and learn about seasonal local produce.
- Create and prepare a recipe for a delicious main dish. Research nutritional value. (Adult supervision)
- Learn how herbs (derived from plants, plant parts) and spices (derived mostly from seeds, berries, bark, plant roots) are used to enhance the flavor of food, and also provide health benefits.

MY KNOWLEDGE PAGE
(INFORMATION, DISCOVERIES, AND QUESTIONS)

Most people can benefit from taking supplements to ensure their body receives the vitamins and minerals it needs.

Cooking vegetables by lightly steaming helps retain valuable nutrients.

I contribute to my body's wellness and energy level by taking time to eat a nutritional breakfast.

What are the nutritional advantages of eating sea vegetables?

Adding lime juice to my drinking water helps to create an acid/alkaline balance in my body.

Name __Author__

Section __Physical__ Lesson __2 – Nutrition__

NOTES TO MYSELF

I need to add more fruit to my present diet.

Take vitamin D supplements on days spent mostly indoors.

I will bless my food and appreciate how it nourishes my body.

Drink small quantities of filtered water throughout the day (room temperature is best).

Check labeling carefully for: natural, organic, certified organic, non-GMO foods.

FACILITATOR NOTES

3. Exercise

Preparation

> Find Internet examples depicting ways people exercise. (Optional)
> Make three Exercise Label cards. Use three index cards and write a heading on each: Flexibility, Aerobic, Anaerobic. Laminate for repeated use.
> Make Exercise Picture cards. Illustrate or glue Internet images of exercise modalities on large index cards. Laminate for repeated use.

Materials

Exercise Label cards, Exercise Picture cards, computer Internet (optional), hula hoops or jump ropes

Presentation

INTRODUCTION—Invite students to explore Exercise, an aspect related to our PHYSICAL SELF. Ask students what they know or think they know about Exercise.

    a. Show Internet Exercise examples (optional). Discuss the important need for exercising our bodies. A sedentary lifestyle creates health risks to the physical body. Proper fitness is essential to our physical health and contributes to our mental/emotional well-being. Studies recommend 45–60 minutes of exercise daily.

    b. Discuss the motivating factors for making a commitment to exercising (e.g., strengthens and tones, improves stamina, reduces stress, helps prevent disease, controls weight).

    c. Explain the three types of exercise: Lay out the Exercise Label cards.
        1. *Flexibility:* yoga, Tai Chi, or exercises that focus on stretching.
        2. *Aerobic:* cycling, skipping rope, or exercises to increase cardiovascular endurance.
        3. *Anaerobic:* weight training, sprinting, or exercises that increase short-term muscle strength.

    d. Present Exercise Picture cards. Have students group cards into flexibility, aerobic, or anaerobic exercises. Place each card under the proper exercise label heading.

    e. Discuss weekly fitness routines that would include the three types of exercise. (It may be important if one has health considerations to consult with a doctor before beginning an exercise program.)

f. Discuss the benefits of taking a daily walk.

g. Explore the various types of sports that students may be involved or have interest in. Discuss the exercise benefits; also the health and safety factors.

h. Practice some warm-up and cool-down stretches. (Work individually or pair-up students to assist each other.)

i. Pass out hula hoops /jump ropes to play with.

CLOSING—Ask students to comment. What questions do they have about Exercise? Questions can be written on their SELF-INQUIRY PAGE for exploration and research.

Name __Author__

Section __Physical__   Lesson __3 – Exercise__

SELF-INQUIRY PAGE

What might be a fun aerobic exercise to try?

How is my posture?

What weight-bearing exercises can I incorporate into my exercise routine?

Is it best to take a walk before or after a meal?

What recreational sports would I enjoy participating in?

3. Exercise

CREATIVE ACTIVITIES

1. Develop a personal fitness program. Make a chart with the days of the week. Write down anaerobic exercises for each day. Include three days of aerobic/cardiovascular exercises each week. Include warm-up/cool-down stretches, and movement/flexibility exercises for both morning and night. Start at your own comfort level or ten minutes a day, working up to the recommended 45—60 minutes daily. Do you prefer to exercise alone or with others? (Materials: paper, pencil, ruler)

2. Learn and practice some eye exercises. How will you incorporate some of these into your exercise routine? (Materials: paper, pencil)

3. Listen to different types of music and move your body to the sounds you hear. What music encourages a cardiovascular workout? (Materials: eclectic samples of dance music (e.g., rock, hip-hop, African, Latin, reggae, classical), technology source)

4. Design an interesting walking hike (about one mile) that begins at your home or school and continues around the neighborhood. Enjoy walking accompanied by friends or family. Can you make your walk more of a full-body workout by using hand weights or walk/sprinting? (Materials: drawing paper, pencil, colored pencils, markers)

5. Invent a couple new yoga poses. What will you name them? Illustrate your poses on index cards and practice them with friends. (Materials: large white index cards, black marker)

Exercise —cont.

Sample illustration by the Author: Activity 4.

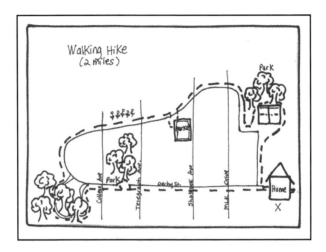

Additional Ideas for Exploration

- Explore the practices of yoga, Tai Chi, and/or Qigong. Get professional recommendations on how to add Eastern elements into your exercise program. Perhaps invite an instructor to give a demonstration. (Upper grades)
- Participate in a new sports activity (e.g., soccer, Frisbee, swimming, softball). Be sure to follow the safety procedures and guidelines. Remember competition is about personal excellence and sportsmanship.
- Create an obstacle course outdoors with friends. Keep safety in mind.
- Make up a dance routine to music you enjoy.
- Read a biography of a famous Olympian. Get inspired to challenge yourself athletically.

MY KNOWLEDGE PAGE
(INFORMATION, DISCOVERIES, AND QUESTIONS)

How beneficial is jogging?

Regular weight-bearing exercises strengthen the bones along with a calcium-rich diet.

Taking time to dance to upbeat music each day is mood-enhancing, and a fun workout.

Tennis is a good weight-bearing exercise that interests me.

It is important to minimize eye strain while using the computer. A recommendation is 20-20-20. Every 20 minutes—look into the distance about 20 feet away—for 20 seconds.

Name _Author_

Section _Physical_   Lesson   3 – Exercise

NOTES TO MYSELF

Take time for gentle stretching during the day.

Practice Salutation To The Sun yoga stances in the morning.

Make an intention for taking a brisk walk (aerobic exercise) every day.

Good posture!

Remember to do warm-ups before vigorous exercise.

FACILITATOR NOTES

4. Rhythm

Preparation

> Create a Human Rhythm poster. Glue photos or illustrations depicting the growth stages of a human on a poster board.

Materials

3D models of the earth and sun (plastic balls can substitute for globes), Human Rhythm poster, white board, dry erase marker, percussion instruments

Presentation

INTRODUCTION—Invite students to explore Rhythm, an aspect related to our PHYSICAL SELF. Ask students what they know or think they know about Rhythm.

a. Have a student demonstrate how the earth and sun move using the models. Our earth is a living organism that has its own rhythmic nature. Each life form on the planet also has its own internal rhythm—seasons for growth and change.

b. Display Human Rhythm poster. Discuss how humans develop and change throughout a typical life cycle.

c. Discuss the rhythmic patterns that our bodies perform for us (e.g. heartbeat, digestion, sleep, blood circulation, menstruation). Our biorhythms are the internal mechanism for these biological functions.

d. Discuss the importance of giving our bodies rest. Attention to sleep/rest habits help to ensure that our body functions properly. Explore activities that support relaxation (e.g. taking a bath, reading, coloring, handcrafts).

e. Explore historical traditions of honoring one's own stages of growth with the cycles of nature. Our ancestors marked seasons of the year with ritual and festivals that transcended any religious ideology. Paying homage to light and life itself in community celebration were most universally observed on the winter and summer solstice (usually December 21 and June 21 in the northern hemisphere). The winter solstice acknowledges the sky, sun, and the sacred masculine principle; the summer solstice is a festival of the earth and the sacred feminine principle.

f. Make a list together on the board of ways people respond to the earth's rhythms (e.g., change in eating and sleeping habits, home décor, outdoor sports, gardening).

    g. Discuss the importance of creating rituals for rites of passage, personal and community renewal, and for celebrating our cycles of growth with the rhythms of nature. Simple rituals can be a spoken word, or include several acts that enhance your awareness of the stages of your day (e.g., before meals, showering, before night's sleep). Imagine ways to create community celebrations incorporating essential elements of music, food, dance, and play.

    h. Create improvisational music using percussion instruments.

CLOSING—Ask students to comment. What questions do they have about Rhythm? Questions can be written on their SELF-INQUIRY PAGE for exploration and research.

Name __Author__

Section __Physical__   Lesson __4 - Rhythm__

SELF-INQUIRY PAGE

What conditions can cause my body to feel stressed?

What phase of the moon is optimal for beginning a new project?

Does my body respond differently during each season (sleep patterns, diet, exercise needs, etc.)?

Do I listen to my body by eating and resting when needed?

What are some simple things I can do to feel rejuvenated?

4. Rhythm

CREATIVE ACTIVITIES

1. Greet a new day! Plan an early morning retreat with your group or family to witness a sunrise. Pack a picnic breakfast and allow yourself time for quiet introspection. What wonderful qualities are beginning to rise within YOU? (Materials: picnic breakfast supplies, blanket)

2. How do you imagine your life to look five years from now? Draw an image of what you would like to be doing. How about one year from now? Draw another image. Do some journal writing with each drawing. (Materials: drawing paper, markers, journal, pen)

3. Relax to soothing music of nature. Find a comfortable place to lie down. Begin to quiet your body by closing your eyes. Focus on your toes. Tighten them and then relax. Move to your ankles and continue up to the face by focusing on each part of the body—tightening and relaxing. Relax and rest for ten minutes. How did your body benefit from this exercise? (Materials: calming sounds of nature, technology source, floor pillows)

4. Pretend you have won a dream vacation! Draw an outline of a large luggage bag on paper. Draw or write inside your bag the many things you would like your ideal dream vacation to include (e.g., beach, sports, theatre, restaurants, sightseeing). Which things are free? Who would you bring on your trip? (Materials: paper, colored pencils, markers)

5. Learn a new handcraft (e.g., sewing, model building, beading, scrapbooking). Do you balance your time spent with family/friends with having some private alone time? (Materials: craft materials as needed)

Rhythm – cont.

Sample illustration by Author: Activity 4.

Additional Ideas for Exploration

- Write down your worries and leave them in a jar. Take a nature walk.
- Make a new positive resolution that you will now begin.
- Dance outside with nature, moving and connecting with your surroundings.
- Draw a picture of yourself relaxing near a body of water.
- Celebrate a rite of passage.

Name _Author_

Section _Physical_   Lesson _4 – Rhythm_

MY KNOWLEDGE PAGE
(INFORMATION, DISCOVERIES, AND QUESTIONS)

The "slow movement" encourages leisurely dining and an overall slower pace of life.

I increase my chances of acquiring a migrane headache by not eating at a regular time, or spending extended time in the sun.

Celebrating the change of seasons with festivals and ritual is a way to show reverance for the earth.

The new moon is an optimal time for beginning a new project.

It is best to sleep in a darkened room. Artifical light at night interferes with natural sleep cycles.

NOTES TO MYSELF

Participate in a solstice ceremony in my community.

Learn about the diverse rituals of other cultures that celebrate life's passages.

Learn more about the earth's electro-magnetic fields that can influence the human body either positively or negatively.

Learn new Dances of Universal Peace.

I will practice slow dining to enjoy my food and the company I share a meal with.

FACILITATOR NOTES

5. Energy Centers

Preparation

> Make an Energy Centers poster. Draw an outline of a human body on a white poster board (or enlarge and trace template). Illustrate the location of the seven major energy centers and their symbols with colored pencils (Internet source).
> Make a Body Outline copy for each student (see template).

Materials

Energy Centers poster, Body Outline copies, colored pencils, book on chakras with visual charts

Presentation

INTRODUCTION—Invite students to explore Energy Centers, an aspect related to our PHYSICAL SELF. Ask students what they know or think they know about Energy Centers.

a. Display Energy Centers poster. Explain some basic facts. There are seven major energy centers (chakras = meaning "wheel" in Sanskrit) of the human energy system. These spinning vortices of energy funnel out the front and back of the body along the spine and up to our crown—*Base, Sacral, Solar Plexus, Heart, Throat, Third Eye, Crown*—receiving, assimilating, and transmitting information with other humans, animals, plants; all life forms. They are associated with the colors of a rainbow: (from bottom to top) red, orange, yellow, green, blue, indigo, and violet. Psychologically, energy centers correspond to areas of ourselves: (from bottom to top) survival, sexuality, power, love, communication, imagination, and spirituality. These spirals of energy differ in size and activity in each of us, being relative to one's ability to integrate their characteristics.

b. Pass out the Body Outline copies. Present the seven major energy centers by referring to book on chakras. Begin with the first energy center (base chakra). Explain basic associations and qualities for each center. Students can color in the energy centers and symbols on their outlines as they are discussed.

c. Discuss how energy centers can become over-energized or under-

51

energized. These changes are dependent on physical, mental, emotional, and spiritual factors that determine our state of health and balance.

d. Discuss how the energy center of the heart is the gateway to awareness and well-being. A major source of dysfunction with humanity is energetically closing the heart due to wounding (e.g., loss of love, betrayal, rejection, prejudice, hatred, numbness). The heart matrix is stronger and more expansive than the matrix of the brain.

e. Explore how we all have the opportunity to learn how to master each energy center's essence and unite them harmoniously. As we become more consciously aware, we integrate the lower chakras associated with fundamental emotions and needs, with the higher frequency centers that relate to heightened mental and spiritual faculties.

f. Practice a guided imagery for cleansing and energizing the seven major energy centers.

Begin at the base. Flood each energy center with the colored light that it is associated with. Simultaneously tone the sound that relates to each center.

CLOSING—Ask students to comment. What questions do they have about Energy Centers? Questions can be written on their SELF-INQUIRY PAGE for exploration and research.

SELF-INQUIRY PAGE

How expansive are the energy centers at birth?

Do any of my major energy centers feel over-energized? Under-energized?

Which energy centers are my emotions directing my awareness to? Why?

How can I further activate the upper energy centers?

What causes me to feel ungrounded?

5. Energy Centers

CREATIVE ACTIVITIES

1. "Tune" into the well-being of your seven major energy centers. What areas of your body feel well-balanced? Are any areas feeling under-energized? Over-energized? Intuitively draw and color a circle design for each major energy center without censoring on a Body Outline (see template). How does this visual inform you? (The body can offer a positive/negative response to questions related to health and well-being by using kinesiology (muscle testing). Use this information for exploring body-mind connections, and to seek healing modalities.) (Materials: Body Outline copy, colored pencils)

2. Pick an energy center that needs balancing. Paint an abstract image of how it presently feels. What does this center want to say to you? Do some journaling about your drawing. Paint another image depicting this energy center glowing with vibrancy. Continue journaling. Use the second image in a visualization to promote healing. (Materials: heavyweight paper, tempera paints, brushes, rags, water container, journal, pen)

3. Look at images of mandala art from many cultures. Notice the balanced-centered design. Take a few minutes in silence to feel centered within yourself, and then begin to paint your own mandala. Begin from the middle of a circle outline. What shapes or symbols will you use in your design? Energize your mandala design by painting it with many values of color. (Materials: book on mandalas, heavyweight paper cut into 12" square, tempera paints, brushes, rags, water container)

4. Learn energy techniques for strengthening your solar plexus area. This is the body's physical center, (called hara in yoga, and dan tien in Qigong). What simple tools can you use routinely? (Materials: book on energy healing)

5. Have an energetic group chakra dance. Acquire music that stimulates the seven major life force centers starting with the base and moving upwards. Allow your body to inform your moves. Which energy areas are the easiest to express? Why is that? Write in your journal about your experience. (Materials: corresponding music for each chakra, technology source, colorful scarves (optional), journal, pen)

Energy Centers – cont.

Sample illustration by the Author: Activity 2.

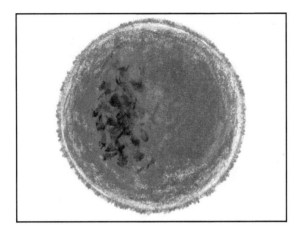

Additional Ideas for Exploration

- Paint a group mural of a magnificent rainbow (a sign of hope).
- Do some research on a modality used for balancing energy centers: color therapy, radical forgiveness, sound, etc.
- Invite a professional Reiki master to your school to explain "attunements."
- Examine your role as either the functional or dysfunctional archetype that relates to the emotional qualities governing each chakra (Internet source). (Upper grades)
- Be appreciative of the amazing design of your physical body and its capabilities.

MY KNOWLEDGE PAGE
(INFORMATION, DISCOVERIES, AND QUESTIONS)

Help balance the first energy center (base or root chakra) by: eating root vegetables, wearing the color red, drinking water from a red colored bottle/ glass that has been exposed to the sun, drumming, and connecting to the earth (as in gardening). This center is associated with issues of survival, home, and finances. It is important to work on grounding oneself when this feels unbalanced.

How can I expand my 6th chakra?

Each energy center corresponds to a specific color, sound, fragrance, mantra, psychological aspect, body organ/organs, etc.

I can open myself up to feel more loving to help activate my upper energy centers. The heart area acts as a bridge between the upper and lower centers.

Universal energy comes in through the crown area of the body. The energy center of the crown vibrates at a high frequency.

NOTES TO MYSELF

Paint mandalas!

My throat energy center feels very expansive. Wearing a blue scarf will help nourish this energy center.

Find out how tuning forks are used to balance energy centers.

The energy center of the heart is the "thinking," "feeling," "knowing," organ of a human.

Research more information about the "positive" and "negative" archetypes associated with the seven major energy centers.

First chakra = mother/ victim

Second chakra = emperor-empress/ martyr

Third chakra = warrior/ servant

Fourth chakra = lover/ actor

Fifth chakra = communicator/ silent child

Sixth chakra = intuitive/ intellectual

Seventh chakra = guru/ egotist

FACILITATOR NOTES

6. Sexuality

Preparation

> Create a People collage. Glue magazine images of people on a poster board. Include people of different ages, ethnicity, and also images of couples.

Materials

People collage

Presentation

INTRODUCTION—Invite students to explore Sexuality, an aspect related to our PHYSICAL SELF. Ask students what they know or think they know about Sexuality.

a. Display People collage.
b. Discuss how humans are sexual beings beginning from birth. Discuss how people have different sexual orientations. Our sexual energy creates a desire for a partner as we mature.
c. Discuss our innate male and female attributes. Every individual carries both male and female attributes that need to come into balance. These attributes are often associated with a certain gender: *Male*—practical, assertive, realistic, etc., *Female*—nurturing, emotional, enduring, etc. Male qualities and traits are normally registered with the left hemisphere of the brain, female qualities normally in the right hemisphere.
d. *Explore the courtship practices of different cultures. *(Upper grades)
e. *Explain the differences of sexual experiences. 1. Sexual intimacy can be a profound sharing of deep feelings of love and tenderness between humans. 2. Sexual activity is a means for pro-creation. 3. Sex can also be a source of physical release without deep emotional connection. (Sexual abuse is non-consensual and does not feel good. This behavior requires professional assistance for intervention and to process the intense feelings that are its result.) *(Upper grades)
f. *Explore safe sex topics (e.g., boundaries, seeking help for abuse, birth control, emotional maturity). (These topics can be further discussed in Activity 3.) *(Upper grades)
g. Remind students of your availability to discuss sensitive issues and

questions in private.

h. Explore how our sexual (creative) energy can be used as fuel for creating positive activity in our lives. Have students share how they are passionately bringing more joy into their life.

CLOSING—Ask students to comment. What questions do they have about Sexuality? Questions can be written on their SELF-INQUIRY PAGE for exploration and research.

SELF-INQUIRY PAGE

Am I embracing the sensual richness of life?

What are now my strongest masculine and feminine qualities?

Have I been using my sexual energy wisely?

What methods of birth control are safe and effective?

Who or what is my muse?

6. Sexuality

CREATIVE ACTIVITIES

1. Think of someone who seems to be confident with their "gender." Journal about how comfortable you are with your sexuality. Are you in need of working on balancing your masculine and feminine aspects? (Materials: journal, pen)

2. Drape pieces of fabric around your shoulders. Experience how the different colors and textures feel. How do they feel different? Which do you prefer? What colors are missing from your wardrobe? (Materials: one-yard pieces of colored fabric of various textures (e.g., wool, satin, terry cloth, silk, cotton, velvet)

3. What "sexy" questions do you have? Create a sexuality forum. (Upper grades) Write down questions anonymously on pieces of paper. Facilitator leads a discussion about topics and questions. (Materials: paper, pencil)

4. Loosen up by moving expressively about the room for several minutes. Begin to paint passionately, allowing energy to move through your dancing hands uninhibited. Cover the paper with abstract movements of color. Are you able to paint freely? (Materials: heavyweight paper, acrylic paints, brushes, rags, water container)

5. Take yourself on a "play date." (Upper grades) What would you wear that makes you feel attractive? Where would you go? What would you enjoy eating? What scents and sounds would you surround yourself with? Create an invitation to yourself. (Materials: paper, colored pencils, markers, rubber stamps, stamp pads, envelope)

Sexuality – cont.

Sample illustration by the Author: Activity 5.

Additional Ideas for Exploration

- Develop proper etiquette and social graces.
- Write in your journal about how you can be a greater lover of life.
- Explore your acceptance level for different gender orientations. Have a group discussion. (Upper grades)
- Appreciate and love your body. You are uniquely beautiful. Learn to enhance your best features.
- Learn to discern who are positive role models for how you dress, care for your body, and present yourself to others.

MY KNOWLEDGE PAGE
(INFORMATION, DISCOVERIES, AND QUESTIONS)

Eroticism = powerful positive pattern
vs. Lust = weak negative pattern.

I am making wise choices now for how I expend
my sexual energy.

Tantra is a spiritual practice with roots in India. A
focus is on the feminine "Shakti" kundalini energy,
and the masculine "Shiva." The union between lovers
can be enhanced to make the act of lovemaking a
Sacred Energy exchange.

Sexuality was not a topic openly discussed when
I was growing up. As a result, I felt embarassed
and uninformed about my sexual identity as a young
adult.

The creative energy from the second chakra allows
me to feel great passion for artistic pursuits.

NOTES TO MYSELF

Feeling comfortable with one's sexuality has less to do with body image and more to do with feeling confident and self-loving.

Intimacy is the experience of connecting on a deep level energetically.

"There comes a time when the risk to remain tight in the bud is more painful than the risk it takes to blossom." – Anais Nin

Be cognizant of gender identification verbiage.

Be sensuous and passionate about this grand adventure called "life."

FACILITATOR NOTES

7. Senses

Preparation

> Prepare sensory food samples. Arrange cut-up foods for sensory stimulation (e.g., oranges, pickles, hot peppers, ginger, lemons) on an attractive plate.

Materials

Five reproductions of famous paintings with diverse styles (e.g., Frida Kahlo, Rembrandt Von Rijn, Mary Cassatt, Jacob Lawrence, Wassily Kandinsky), sample styles of music, technology source, sensory food samples, napkins, paper, pencils

Presentation

INTRODUCTION—Invite students to explore Senses, an aspect related to our PHYSICAL SELF. Ask students what they know or think they know about Senses.

a. Discuss how what we *see, hear, taste, smell,* and *touch* affects each of us in different ways. We are attracted to or repelled by sensory experiences based on our constitution, emotional experiences, and cultural conditioning.

b. Explain how we all have a "sixth sense" called *intuition*. This "gut feeling" can be developed with attention.

c. Give each student paper to write down their responses during a sensory exploration. Ask students to notice how their bodies react when presented with the following:

    A. Paintings: Show each work separately.

    B. Music: Play short excerpts from various styles.

    C. Food: Offer sensory food samples to smell and taste.

d. Have students describe their sensory responses.

e. Ask students how they would match the food and music with each style of painting. Have students share which group they resonate with most.

f. Discuss the importance of monitoring what we ingest sensorally by our choices of food, computer games, movies, television programs, books, music, etc. These choices can raise or lower our life force energy levels.

g. Invite students to recall a positive sensory experience; and another that was harder on the body to "digest."

CLOSING—Ask students to comment. What questions do they have about Senses? Questions can be written on their SELF-INQUIRY PAGE for exploration and research.

SELF-INQUIRY PAGE

How do our senses change as we grow and mature?

How can I enhance the sensory elements in my home?

Why is it that people of different generations develop their own style of music?

What sounds to I love? Detest?

What smells conjure up strong memories?

7. Senses

CREATIVE ACTIVITIES

1. Does your body language convey what you want to say to others? Your body is a strong communicator. Notice what parts of your body "speak" loudly and which "communicate" softly. Do some journaling. (Materials: journal, pen)

2. Go on a sensory walk in nature with a friend. Try closing your eyes part of the way, allowing your friend to quietly lead you. Be sensitive to smells, sounds, and textures. Make a drawing describing your experience. Which senses were most acute? (Materials: drawing paper, crayons, colored pencils)

3. What sounds do you love? What are your favorite scents? Create a columned chart of the five basic senses. Make "favorite" illustrations on your chart for each sense. (Materials: drawing paper, ruler, colored pencils)

4. Trust your intuition. Our intuition is the sixth sense. Journal about times you have allowed your sixth sense to guide you. How did you receive this information in your body? (Materials: journal, pen)

5. Experience the sensation from small containers filled with familiar scents (e.g., pine needles, beach sand, baby powder, dirt, coffee grinds, lavender, sage, etc.). What memories do they evoke? Make a painting of a particularly strong image that comes to mind. Do some journaling with your image. (Materials: heavyweight paper, tempera paints, brushes, rags, water container, journal, pen)

Senses –cont.

Sample illustration by the Author: Activity 2.

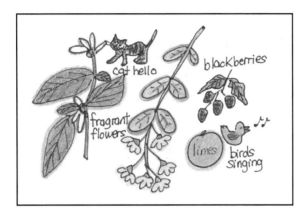

Additional Ideas for Exploration

- Try tasting an unexplored ethnic cuisine for lunch.
- Stop and tune in to what your body is experiencing a couple times during the day.
- Create a sensory art installation with friends using a refrigerator-size box. Use color, texture, sound, taste, and scent to stimulate a certain mood.
- Wake up in the morning to classical music.
- Visit a new place and experience it with "extra-sensory" perception.

MY KNOWLEDGE PAGE
(INFORMATION, DISCOVERIES, AND QUESTIONS)

Taste buds decline with age resulting in a diminished appetite and a need to use extra salt or sugar for taste.

I like the smell of coffee and autumn leaves. Coffee fragrance reminds me of my mother and her morning ritual of drinking from a special white cup. The fragrances of autumn conjure up the memory of my dad raking large piles of oak leaves from our yard in Connecticut.

What are our innate psychic senses? Why are these qualities not very apparent in most people?

Some of my favorite sounds are: babies giggling, rustling leaves, ocean waves, wind chimes, the chirping of birds, and the music of harps.

Our intuition can be enhanced by listening to the body, meditating, and learning to trust oneself.

NOTES TO MYSELF

Odors from chemical-based cleaning products make me feel ill!

Hang a beautiful relaxing landscape picture on a bedroom wall.

Try eating new ethnic foods seasoned with spices.

Fresh flowers will add uplifting energy to my living space.

Learn to identify the sounds of birds that reside near me.

FACILITATOR NOTES

8. Bodywork

Preparation

> Find Internet examples depicting bodywork demonstrations. (Optional)

Materials

Computer Internet (optional)

Presentation

INTRODUCTION—Invite students to explore Bodywork, an aspect related to our PHYSICAL SELF. Ask students what they know or think they know about Bodywork.

a. Explore the benefits of bodywork. A massage therapist, for example, works on a client's body by administering therapeutic applications. Massage or manipulations applied to specific areas of the body are helpful in treating many ailments and to manage chronic pain. Many professional bodyworkers will also include energy work techniques such as breathwork, emotional release techniques, visualization, etc. in a session.

b. Show Internet Bodywork examples (optional). (Consider asking a professional bodyworker from your community to come talk with students.)

c. Discuss the importance of educating oneself on "alternative" health practices such as bodywork. Alternative health practices/medicine use a holistic approach to health based on natural or traditional methods. There can be certain advantages to exploring alternative options over conventional treatments in terms of expense, safety, and results.

d. Invite students to practice self-massage techniques for the face and scalp. Have students sit on the floor in a circle and practice the following sequence.
Face and Scalp Massage: *Lightly stroke the entire face with your fingers. Stroke from the center of the forehead out to the temples, from the nose to the ears, and from the mouth to edge of the jaw. Use a circular finger motion on the temples. Squeeze with the thumb and index finger all around the ears. Cup hands over the ears and make a circular motion. Place palms on the side of head and circle ten times one-way and*

reverse ten times. Pat with fingers gently all around the eyes. Squeeze eyebrows gently. Tap gently all around your scalp. Gently tug small twisted bunches of hair.

e. Conclude with students in a circle turning to the person on their right and giving a back rub. Use strokes, pressure, or gentle kneading for several minutes. Reciprocate by turning to the person on the left and repeat. (Facilitators need to use discernment in "touching" for some groups. Massaging their own hands and feet is an alternative suggestion.)

CLOSING—Ask students to comment. What questions do they have about Bodywork? Questions can be written on their SELF-INQUIRY PAGE for exploration and research.

SELF-INQUIRY PAGE

What types of bodywork could be most beneficial for me now?

What does a chiropractor do?

Can I give myself a reflexology treatment?

What kinds of bodywork are recommended for children, and elders?

Is there a bodywork training center nearby that offers discounted services to the public?

8. Bodywork

CREATIVE ACTIVITIES

1. Did you know that your mind is a bodywork tool? Practice an energy healing. Ground the body by imagining a cord from the base of your spine going into the earth. Visualize discordant energy flowing out from your feet and into the neutralizing earth. Give yourself a new grounding cord and fill your body with gold suns coming through your crown center. Compile other information on energy work that can assist you every day. (Materials: book on energy tools, paper, pencil)

2. Give yourself a rejuvenating ten-minute chair massage by learning some basic techniques. Where do you feel tension? Indicate on a Body Outline (see template) where your body tends to hold stress. Use this information as a reference for bodywork. (Materials: book on basic massage, Body Outline copy, colored pencils)

3. Explore the basic steps of foot reflexology and practice on yourself. What areas are sensitive to pressure? What body organ is associated with that area? (Materials: book on foot reflexology)

4. View a chart of the body's pressure points (Internet source). Learn how to stimulate energy in needed areas with gentle taps or pressure. Can you give yourself a full-body wake-up treatment? (Materials: chart on acupressure points)

5. How is your posture? Make a note to check your posture throughout the day. Do you have a habit of slumping your shoulders? Learn the proper way to pick up and carry heavy objects. (Materials: none)

Bodywork –cont.

Sample illustration by the Author: Activity 2.

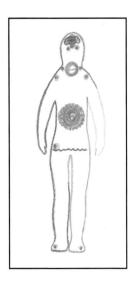

Additional Ideas for Exploration

- Learn about hot stone massage.
- Listen and revitalize to the tones of singing-bowls.
- Study human anatomy.
- Activate pressure points near the base of the skull. Put two tennis balls inside a large sock and knot the end. Lie down on the floor and place the sock underneath the base of your head. Relax in this position for ten minutes.
- Experience a professional bodywork treatment. (Upper grades)

Name __Author__

Section __Physical__   Lesson __8 - Bodywork__

MY KNOWLEDGE PAGE
(INFORMATION, DISCOVERIES, AND QUESTIONS)

Hands and feet have pressure points that correlate to organs in the body.

A full-body massage would help to loosen tension and stiff joints in my body.

A chiropractor uses adjustments and manipulation to relieve impediments to the spinal column. Imbalances can disturb the nervous system.

Reflexology helps to improve circulation, remove toxins, normalize gland function, and strengthen the immune system.

Massage therapy is beneficial for elders because it improves circulation, is relaxing, helps with pain relief, and gives one an overall sense of well-being.

Name _Author_

Section _Physical_   Lesson _8 – Bodywork_

NOTES TO MYSELF

Craniosacral therapy helps to relieve traumatic energy blockages stored in the body.

Give myself a chair massage after studying.

Make an appointment with a professional reflexologist.

Include a chiropractor on my wellness support team.

Save money to indulge in a spa experience!

FACILITATOR NOTES

9. Environment

Preparation

> Rearrange the room environment so that it feels "chaotic." Move furnishings and supplies to create a cluttered and disorganized environment.

Materials

Map of the universe, map of your town/community, book on feng shui

Presentation

INTRODUCTION—Invite students to explore Environment, an aspect related to our PHYSICAL SELF. Ask students what they know or think they know about Environment.

    a. Show the universe map. Discuss our relationship with the environment of Earth and the energy surrounding us in the universe.

    b. Show the community map. Discuss how the environment of our local community affects us.

    c. Ask students how the room environment they are in feels.

    d. Have students reflect about their own personal living spaces at home. Explain how our outer world is often a reflection of how we are feeling.

    e. Have students assist you to arrange furnishings back to a comfortable position. Discuss how changes in our environment can be advantageous to our sense of well-being. Explore ways to further enhance the room.

    f. Discuss basic energy principles of feng shui: meaning attributed to the placement of objects, use of natural elements. The energetic placement of objects in a room can impact us positively or negatively. The five elements of wood, fire, earth, metal, and water can add balance to one's life when incorporated into our living spaces. Share illustrations from the book on feng shui.

    g. Ask students what ideal natural environment they would gravitate to for reflection and inspiration (e.g., a forest, by the ocean, near a mountain). Explore ways to surround one's own bedroom with elements that capture the essence of each response.

    h. Explore ways to create healthy ecological environments in our homes and communities.

i. Encourage students to consider their roles as stewards of the Earth.

CLOSING—Ask students to comment. What questions do they have about Environment? Questions can be written on their SELF-INQUIRY PAGE for exploration and research.

SELF-INQUIRY PAGE

Is my home environment healthy (non-toxic, uncluttered, comfortable)?

How can I use color in my living space to elevate my mood?

Is the lighting in my home adequate and beneficial?

What feng shui principles can I utilize to enhance the energy in my study area?

What are some ways to conserve more energy in my home?

9. Environment

CREATIVE ACTIVITIES

1. Find a spot in your community that can use some sprucing up. (Permission may be needed for public spaces.) How can you beautify this area? Can you start or add to a flower garden? (Materials: gloves, trash bags, rakes, materials as needed)

2. Take an inventory of potentially dangerous or unhealthy elements (e.g., chemical agents in furniture, dust, mold, chipped paint, clogged air ducts, mildew, blown electrical outlets) in a living or workspace. What changes can be made to decrease toxicity in your home environment? What eco-friendly, non-toxic products can be used for household cleaning and pest control? (Materials: paper, pencil)

3. Create recycled art. Use odds and ends of found objects to create a unique work of art. What will you name this piece? (Materials: found objects, scissors, string, masking tape, white glue, hot glue gun, hot glue sticks, materials as needed)

4. Make an Earth art shrine. Stand in a circle with friends outside in a natural setting. Join hands. At the sound of a chime, slowly begin to separate from the group and meander silently, paying close attention to everything in your surroundings. Notice the subtle play of light. Feel the wind and ground that supports you. Let your heart open in gratitude to the elements earth, air, fire, and water. Take your time and begin to see gifts of nature that can be placed in a group collaborative art piece. (Facilitator will secure a place for making this shrine.) After it is complete, participants can have the opportunity to say a word of thanks, sing a song, recite a prayer, or share feelings in the moment. How do you think the piece will change in the next few days? Conclude with an earth blessing. (Materials: chime, nature materials as needed)

5. Draw or write about an ideal bedroom/living space. What elements of feng shui can you incorporate? What elements can you apply to your own bedroom now? (Materials: drawing paper, ruler, pencil, colored pencils)

Environment –cont.

Sample illustration by the Author: Activity 5.

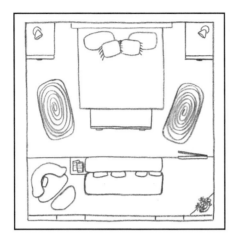

Additional Ideas for Exploration

- Become an environmental activist. Get involved with others to take action toward a passionate cause. (Upper grades)
- Help revamp a room in your home by painting it a new color.
- Unclutter an area in your home/school and reorganize.
- Get greener. Recycle, reuse, rot, and reduce.
- Visit a National Park, or draw your own postcards of natural attractions. Share some interesting research.

MY KNOWLEDGE PAGE
(INFORMATION, DISCOVERIES, AND QUESTIONS)

Cleaning out one's cellar and/or attic contributes to a psychological effect of feeling more relaxed, focused, and positive.

Feng shui suggestions for a study: clutter-free, high-back chair, picture symbolizing water behind chair, window left of desk, wind chime in window, cactus and bamboo plants.

Biotechnology = technology based on biology that can be perceived as "good" or "bad" depending on one's personal beliefs and opinions.

Every individual must take responsibility for taking care of the earth which provides all of us with basic resources to live.

Respect the earth by not littering. Dispose of all trash responsibly.

NOTES TO MYSELF

Paint walls of my living space with muted colors. Accent rooms with colorful paintings, flowers, textured pillows, etc.

To create a feng shui water element in my home I can place a bowl of water on a shelf, or install a small, bubbling fountain.

Clean up and enhance my own neighborhood.

Dispose of batteries and electronics properly.

Sustainability and stewardship protect Mother Earth's future!

FACILITATOR NOTES

10. Breath

Preparation
> Arrange floor pillows for students in a circle. (Optional)

Materials
Floor pillows (optional), diagram explaining human respiration (Internet source),

Presentation
INTRODUCTION—Invite students to explore the Breath, an aspect related to our PHYSICAL SELF. Ask students what they know or think they know about the Breath.

a. Show respiration diagram. Discuss breath as our vital life force. The inhalation and exhalation of the breath oxidizes the food we eat into fuel for every cell in our body. The breath purges toxins from the body.
b. Explain *shallow* (chest) versus *full breath* (abdominal) breathing. Demonstrate the difference. Shallow breathing stops at the chest; full breath (or deep breathing) fills the lower lobes of the lung and involves the movement of the diaphragm on the inhale, massaging abdominal organs.
c. Explain how proper breathing is a building block for good health. Slow and rhythmic deep breathing (approximately 8–10 breaths per minute) eliminates toxins (carbon dioxide waste) more efficiently than shallow breathing. Proper breathing gets more fresh oxygen to the brain and muscles, helping the body perform better mentally and physically.
d. Discuss how our respiration changes under varying circumstances (e.g., fear, sorrow, anger, exertion).
e. Practice an exercise to understand the benefits of good breathing. Good breathing is done through the lower torso, each breath expanding the belly, lower back, and ribs.

Lie down and place your hands on your stomach. Breathe in and out through the nose with long, slow breaths (8–10 breaths a minute is ideal). Feel the nourishing life force enter your lungs, and stale air leaving your body. Relax and breathe in this way for three minutes.

f.   Practice three rejuvenating breathing techniques.

1. Deep breathing: (diaphragmatic breathing) *Expand the diaphragm on the inhale, slowly taking in as much air as you can into the lungs—hold—then exhale, contracting the diaphragm fully as you release air slowly.*

2. Earth breathing: *Inhale from the bottom of your feet up through your crown. Exhale down to your feet and continue breathing in this circular motion.*

3. Yogic nostril breathing: *Inhale slowly (count of 8) through right nostril by closing off left nostril with right ring finger. Exhale slowly (count of 8) through left nostril by closing off right nostril with right thumb. Begin next inhale with same nostril closed off and exhale opposite, continuing for at least three rounds.*

CLOSING—Ask students to comment. What questions do they have about the Breath? Questions can be written on their SELF-INQUIRY PAGE for exploration and research.

Name __Author__

Section __Physical__   Lesson __10 – Breath__

SELF-INQUIRY PAGE

How often am I breathing efficiently?

How do deep breathing techniques promote health?

How can I increase the air quality in my living or work environment?

What happens inside my body as I breathe?

How much oxygen does the average human need each day?

10. Breath

CREATIVE ACTIVITIES

1. Research information about the air quality of where you live. Determine if the air quality in and around your home and/or school is at safe levels. What can be done to improve the air quality in these spaces? (Materials: paper, pencil)

2. Go on a hike in a wooded area with your group. Sense your breathing as you feel the clean air and energy of the trees. Find a large tree and stand close to it with your arms hugging the trunk—connect and breathe into it. How do you feel? Take some time to sit with your back against the tree in silent reverence. What story does this "elder teacher" share? (Materials: walking shoes, first aid kit)

3. Paint a picture of a plant with watercolor paints. Wet your paper. Begin from the base of your plant by painting the roots. Take your time and breathe deeply, oxygenating your body as you paint the stem upwards. Allow the watercolors to make interesting effects. Continue and paint any branches and leaves. Will your plant be flowering? Use your imagination to create your own details. Use this image to meditate on for revitalizing your physical body. (Materials: watercolor paper, watercolor set, brushes, rags, water container)

4. Find a place in a natural setting where you can feel comfortable vocalizing. What sounds want to emerge? Do you suffer with breathing problems? Allow buried sounds to come forward. Vocalize to the elements surrounding you (e.g., trees, insects, rocks, plants, water). Write in your journal about what the sounds convey. (Materials: journal, pen)

5. Visit a blooming flower garden or nursery. What flower fragrances are most appealing to you? Breathe in the colors and essences. Pot a plant and gift it to someone anonymously. (Materials: materials as needed)

Breath –cont.

Sample illustration by the Author: Activity 3.

Additional Ideas for Exploration

- Face the direction of east in the early morning. Close eyes and breathe in "prana."
- Learn and practice some Hatha yoga postures, remembering to focus on the breath.
- Practice vocal exercises.
- Dedicate a newly planted sapling to someone special in your life.
- Take a deep relaxing breath *now*. Slowly breathe in through the nose...and out the mouth.

MY KNOWLEDGE PAGE
(INFORMATION, DISCOVERIES, AND QUESTIONS)

Sighing or yawning is a sign that the body is not getting enough oxygen.

The adult human body requires 88 lbs. of oxygen a day.

Abdominal breathing (deep breathing) is more efficient than thoracic (shallow breathing). Adults tend to do more shallow breathing, while children tend to breathe from the abdomen.

The body removes waste products by: feces 3%, urine 7%, skin 20%, and breath...70%!

The air quality in my house can be improved by adding certain plants to help filter the air: Boston fern, Spider plant = assist to eliminate formaldehyde. English ivy, Peace ivy = assist to eliminate formaldehyde, xylene, and toluene.

NOTES TO MYSELF

Develop optimal breathing habits.

Have the air quality in my home tested.

Walk, ride a bike, and use public transportation often.

Invest in adding indoor plants that are aesthetically pleasing, and help to filter the air.

Circular breathing – (lying down and breathing in and out through the mouth) releases challenging feelings. Visualize golden light entering the body after this process.

FACILITATOR NOTES

Section II:
The MENTAL SELF

The
MENTAL
SELF

ENERGY / The Mental Body / CREATIVITY

Our mental self comprises the intellect and its potential to express wisdom. The mental body is an energy system of the mind. Let's explore the Mental Self and its related aspects through the creative process.

Here are some FACTS about our MENTAL SELF:
- The human brain weighs about three pounds.
- Our culture has primarily focused on linguistic and logical mathematical intelligence.
- The brain has two cerebral hemispheres each of which specializes in certain behaviors.
- Omega-3 EFA (essential fatty acid) is necessary for brain health.
- Only 12% of people dream in black and white.
- The mind is a vast source of super power.
- The brain requires more oxygen than any other organ, 20% of what the entire body needs.
- The mental power of our beliefs will program our lives either "positively" or "negatively."
- The brain has many nerve cells, but no pain receptors.
- Our intelligence gives us the ability to perceive opportunities around us.

The Mental Self

1. Mind
2. Learning Styles
3. Language
4. Information
5. Memory
6. Consciousness
7. Thought
8. Choice
9. Wisdom
10. Ideas

1. Mind

Preparation

> Make a Left-brain/Right-brain poster. List the characteristics of left and right brain functions on a white poster board (Internet source).

Materials

Human brain illustration depicting its three layers (Internet source), human brain illustration depicting the two hemispheres (Internet source), Left-brain/Right-brain poster, computer Internet

Presentation

INTRODUCTION—Invite students to explore the Mind, an aspect related to our MENTAL SELF. Ask students what they know or think they know about the Mind.

    a. Discuss the qualities of the mind. The mind is associated with our intellectual capacity to think, perceive, feel, and reason.

    b. Explore the difference between the terms brain and mind. The terms brain and mind are often used interchangeably but are in fact two distinct concepts that function together. The *brain* is a biochemical organ, a vessel in which electronic impulses create thought. The *mind* refes often to the thought processes of reason, conscience, and awareness of things. Our mind has expansive potential.

    c. Show the human brain illustration. Explain the three layers of the human brain. 1. <u>Brain Stem</u>: (reptilian brain) The innermost layer where essential body functions are controlled—digestion, circulation, respiration, natural healing. 2. <u>Limbic System</u>: (mammalian brain) The middle layer and domain for emotion and appetites—food, sex. 3. <u>Neo-Cortex</u>: (human brain) The outermost layer is youngest in evolution and the seat of human intelligence.

    d. Show the human brain illustration depicting the two hemispheres. The two hemispheres of the neo-cortex communicate by a web of nerve fibers called the corpus callosum. The left side of the brain controls muscles on the right side of the body; the right side of the brain controls the left side of the body.

e. Present Left-brain/Right-brain poster. Neuroscience has demonstrated that we have a natural inclination toward the processes of one side of the brain. The *left side* is considered analytical, logical, and sequential. The *right side* is described as being abstract, intuitive, and holistic. (Our culture's present right-brain dominant Conceptual Age has superseded the Information Age characterized by left-brain thinking. Qualities such as ingenuity, empathy, and global insight will now be favored.) Invite students to take a Left/Right brain test on the Internet.

f. Practice a couple of brain balancing exercises. Drink some water before and after these exercises to help transmit energy across the two hemispheres.

Exercise 1. Tap the back of your hand at the "V" between the knuckles of your little and ring finger while you follow these steps: Close your eyes. Open your eyes. Hold your head still and look to the left; then to the right. Hold your head still and circle your eyes 360° clockwise, then circle counterclockwise. Hum a tune. Count aloud from one to five. Hum a tune.

Exercise 2. Tap on the outside edges of your eyebrows while you follow these steps: Close your eyes. Open your eyes. Move your eyes in a horizontal figure eight (infinity sign). Count aloud from one to five. Hum a tune. Count aloud from one to five.

g. Explore the power of the mind in creating our lives. Our minds give us our sense of cognition and beingness (conscious awareness). We can choose to be more conscious of our thoughts and use the mind to imagine our dreams.

h. Invite students to sit quietly and visualize being plugged into an infinite source of power. Reflect on how powerful we are in positively affecting everything we focus our attention on.

CLOSING—Ask students to comment. What questions do they have about the Mind? Questions can be written on their SELF-INQUIRY PAGE for exploration and research.

SELF-INQUIRY PAGE

What will the collective mind believe in the distant future?

What does the phrase "mind over matter" signify?

How can I increase my level of intelligence?

What does new brain research demonstrate?

How can I boost my left-brain skills?

1. Mind

CREATIVE ACTIVITIES

1. Draw an abstract image to show what is currently occupying your mind. Journal with your image. How would this image feel if you were to live inside it? Are your thoughts contributing to feelings of doom and gloom, or hope and joy? (Materials: drawing paper, crayons, markers, journal, pen)

2. Practice being "mindful' while doing an everyday task such as folding clothes, cleaning a room, eating a meal, etc. Can you practice being mindful throughout the day? When is it more challenging to be mindful? What did you notice about yourself? Write in your journal. (Materials: journal, pen)

3. Try Superbrain Yoga once or twice a day—a technique developed by Master Choa Kok Sui. Connect tongue to palate. Face east. Cross your right arm over your left arm, placing thumbs on front of earlobes and other fingers behind ears. Squat on an inhale breath 14—21 times, exhaling as you rise. Try adding this exercise to your daily morning routine. Do you notice an increase in your ability to focus? (Materials: none)

4. Paint a landscape on thin cardboard that has been primed with gesso. Cut up your painting into about fifty puzzle pieces when it is dry. Put it back together. Which process was more enjoyable? (Materials: thin cardboard (about 11" x 14"), gesso, acrylic paints, brushes, rags, water container)

5. What geometric shapes are you most attracted to? Study geometry. Learn to draw some colorful geometric patterns. Explore sacred geometry symbols such as the yin-yang, star tetrahedron, torus, flower of life, etc. (Materials: book on geometric designs, drawing paper, pencil, ruler, eraser, colored pencils)

Mind –cont.

Sample illustration by Author: Activity 1.

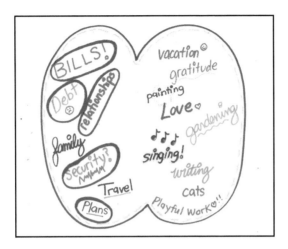

Additional Ideas for Exploration

- Boost left-brain skills by making up a sequential math word problem or crossword puzzle for your friends to solve.

- Study the theory of intelligences by Howard Gardner. Work to develop ALL of the "intelligences," not just the ones you excel at.

- Enjoy scribbling with crayons on paper. Try using your non-dominant hand.

- Read about the historical life of someone considered to have been a "great mind." Dress-up as your character and comment on life in the twenty-first century.

- Go stargazing and learn about the constellations. You, like the stars, exist in a field of infinite possibilities.

MY KNOWLEDGE PAGE
(INFORMATION, DISCOVERIES, AND QUESTIONS)

The collective mind has generally been driven by an illusion of power, and materialism.

Carl Jung recognized the "mother" as the primordial archetype of the collective mind. Our civilization rose from a Neolithic culture that honored the mother goddess. Over time, the West has rejected the matriarchal aspect of the collective consciousness (which respected the balance of the sacred feminine and masculine), and developed a patriarchal society.

Critical Brain connections in young children that determine emotional, social, and intellectual development are influenced by positive affection from parents and caregivers.

The brain grows and continues to develop throughout one's life if the right conditions are met (diet, stimulation, etc.).

Universal life force energy ("prana" or "chi") can be directed downwards to the neo-cortex causing neurons to "fire." This activates brain cells for new abilities such as higher IQ, innate psychic abilities, and other potentials. Meditation facilitates this process.

NOTES TO MYSELF

Practice mindfulness when taking a walk.

Taking time to sit in silence lifts my consciousness and affords peace of mind, along with other health benefits.

Resist the illusions of life. Live within a field of infinite possibilities.

My mind can be a fountain of joy, or a source of anguish creating misery and struggle.

I can work on brainteasers and word problems to build my brain function in the left hemisphere.

FACILITATOR NOTES

2. Learning Styles

Preparation

> Make a Learning Styles poster. Draw two vertical lines to make three columns of equal size on a poster board. Make a heading for each column: Visual, Auditory, Kinesthetic. Put five Velcro tabs on the poster under each heading.

> Make Learning Style Characteristics cards. Cut fifteen strips of white paper (about 1 1/2" wide and length of column.) Write five characteristics on the strips for each learning style (Internet source). Laminate for repeated use. Put Velcro tabs on the back of each strip.

> Acquire a questionnaire to determine learning style (Internet source). Make a copy for each student.

Materials

Learning Styles poster, Learning Style Characteristic cards, questionnaire copies, pencils

Presentation

INTRODUCTION—Invite students to explore Learning Styles, an aspect related to our MENTAL SELF. Ask students what they know or think they know about Learning Styles.

a. Discuss learning styles and how people process information best either by seeing, hearing, or experiencing. Most individuals possess a preferred learning style: *visual, auditory,* or *kinesthetic*; however, some people have a combination.

b. Display Learning Styles poster. Have students take turns picking a Learning Style Characteristic card and placing it in the appropriate space on the poster. Explain the characteristics.

c. Have students complete the questionnaire to determine their learning style.

d. Discuss how students can improve study habits by knowing their learning style.

   1. *Visual learners:* learn best by being shown—benefiting from notes, diagrams, and pictures.

2. _Auditory learners:_ learn best by hearing—benefiting from recordings, reading aloud, and music.
3. _Kinesthetic learners:_ learn best by action—benefiting from hands-on, tactile approaches.

e. Have students write down useful study aids for their style on the back of their paper.

f. Discuss and compare conventional teaching/learning methods to experiential teaching/learning. _Conventional_ teaching is based on transferring knowledge/skills. The purpose is directed toward meeting organizational needs or measurable standards. _Experiential_ learning is a "hands-on," learner-based approach that encourages a person's unique growth. The purpose is directed toward personal development, and the individual controls the learning.

g. Brainstorm ways to improve the study of your favorite subject. Discuss ideas that a teacher might use.

CLOSING—Ask students to comment. What questions do they have about Learning Styles? Questions can be written on their SELF-INQUIRY PAGE for exploration and research.

SELF-INQUIRY PAGE

How do I learn best?

Why is experiential learning so powerful?

How diverse are the learning styles of the students in my classroom?

How can I increase my auditory learning?

Can primary learning styles change during the course of one's life?

2. Learning Styles

CREATIVE ACTIVITIES

1. Make some study aids based on your primary learning style to assist you in a specific academic area (e.g., flashcards, outline, recording notes). What helps you to learn best? (Materials: paper, pencil, materials as needed)

2. Explore learning styles by drawing the same object three ways.
First: Draw a still-life object after feeling it while blindfolded (kinesthetic learning).
Second: Draw the same object (without looking at it), by following directions that are given verbally (auditory learning).
Third: Draw the object by looking at it closely (visual learning).
Which process was difficult/easy? (Materials: still-life objects (or flower in a vase), blindfold, drawing paper, pencil, colored pencils)

3. Create a "lesson plan" for a favorite subject area using an experiential learning approach. Review the principles of the process. Present your activity to the other students. What feedback do you receive? (Materials: paper, pencil, materials as needed)

4. Write a story in the perspective of a wild animal. What learning style do you mostly depend upon for survival? Describe a typical day and how a specific learning style assists you. Make an illustration for your story. How has this experience informed you? (Materials: paper, pencil, drawing paper, crayons, colored pencils)

5. Present a five-minute instructional demonstration to your group using simple props (e.g., hemming a pair of pants, animal care, changing a bike tire, how to budget money). How well did they understand the directions? What changes can you make in order for your entire audience to comprehend fully? (Materials: paper, pencil, materials as needed)

Learning Styles – cont.

Sample illustration by the Author: Activity 2.

Additional Ideas for Exploration

- Take a field trip to a local science museum. Be curious.
- Research ways to improve your non-dominant learning styles.
- Try listening to the radio in place of watching movies for one week.
- Have a Scrabble game night with your family.
- Learn a ballroom dance with your group either by watching a video, or from a guest instructor.

MY KNOWLEDGE PAGE
(INFORMATION, DISCOVERIES, AND QUESTIONS)

I am primarily a visual learner.

Writing notes and using diagrams helps me to remember information from lectures and audio recordings.

Teachers/facilitators using experiential approaches can engage students of various learning styles.

Dominant auditory learners are often musically talented, have a well-developed vocabulary, and can learn foreign languages easily.

Kinesthetic learners need to move. Letting a student tap a leg, bounce a foot, sit on a pillow that allows movement, type notes, etc., are ways to address the needs of this type of learner in a classroom.

NOTES TO MYSELF

Use metaphor and imagery as tools to enhance the learning process.

Find an interesting talk radio program. Make a point to tune in regularly.

Take piano lessons.

Help educators to implement new experiential learning strategies into their curriculum.

Let the focus be on the learner directing his/her own growth and development.

FACILITATOR NOTES

3. Language

Preparation

> Make a Greeting poster. Write the words for "hello" in many different languages on a poster board (Internet source).

Materials

Greeting poster, copies of a popular picture storybook in several languages, Pictionary game (Optional)

Presentation

INTRODUCTION—Invite students to explore Language, an aspect related to our MENTAL SELF. Ask students what they know or think they know about Language.

    a. Discuss the history of language. Primitive pictures and sounds were first used for communication, which then evolved to written languages and diverse dialects. The study of language is called linguistics. Studies show that there are more than 6,500 spoken languages in the world, although many are only spoken by a small population.

    b. Ask students what languages they understand. Show the storybooks.

    c. Display Greeting poster. Practice saying the different sounds for the same word meaning.

    d. Discuss the power of the spoken word. The words we speak are powerful energy vibrations, especially when delivered with a strong feeling tone. Every word we speak (and also what we think) affects other humans, animals, plants, and the elements on a psychic level.

    e. Discuss ways humans communicate with their body posture and facial expressions. We send messages to others through our body language.

    f. Explore cultural differences in body language. These differences may show up in a number of ways, such as in displaying physical touch (e.g., In Italy, a person is often greeted with a hug and kiss on both cheeks; rather in Japan a respectable bow is appropriate). The comfortable conversational distance between people, as well as the interaction between genders may also differ in cultures.

    g. Explore the language of our pets and how they tell us what they are feeling. (Cats and dogs have distinct behaviors for communicating, for example.)

h. Discuss how computer technology has opened up new ways to bridge communication between cultures. It is its own developing language.

i. Discuss how music and art are universal languages.

j. Play Pictionary or charades with your group.

CLOSING—Ask students to comment. What questions do they have about Language? Questions can be written on their SELF-INQUIRY PAGE for exploration and research.

SELF-INQUIRY PAGE

What are some easy methods for increasing my vocabulary?

How engaging is my communication style?

What foreign language would I like to study?

How clearly do I speak?

How can I improve my body language and listening skills so as to communicate being "present" with others?

3. Language

CREATIVE ACTIVITIES

1. Tell a friend about a memorable birthday by speaking only gibberish. How well were you understood by intonation and body language? (Materials: none)

2. Read a favorite children's book and then retell the story to a friend in your own words. Use props from a "story bag" to add interest. Have the friend tell you how engaged they were with your storytelling. How easy was it to imagine the story from your description? How clearly was the plot understood? (Materials: children's book, story bag with props)

3. Recite a poem into a recorder and play it back. How was your speech? Can you improve on your delivery and enunciation? (Materials: book of poems, recording device)

4. Power-up your vocabulary with new words you hear or read. Write the words with their definitions on index cards for review. How can you practice using a new word in conversation the next few days? (Materials: index cards, pencil)

5. Compose a story, poem, or illustrate a wise saying by using only magazine images glued on paper. How well do the images convey your message? (Materials: heavyweight paper (18" x 24"), magazines, scissors, glue sticks, markers)

Language – cont.

Sample illustration by the Author: Activity 5.

Additional Ideas for Exploration

- Learn to sing a favorite song in a foreign language.
- Spend a day at your local library.
- Explore family dynamics by looking at the body language displayed in photographs.
- Make a doodle diary. Draw images of your day and how you feel.
- Avoid idle chatter. Practice speaking only to improve on the silence.

MY KNOWLEDGE PAGE
(INFORMATION, DISCOVERIES, AND QUESTIONS)

It has been estimated that there are approximately between 6,500 and 6,900 living languages in the world. Studies show that many of these are spoken by fewer than 1,000 speakers. Mandarin Chinese is the most popular language.

Eye contact and a relaxed body posture will improve communication as well as other active listening skills. Paraphrasing, clarification, and obtaining feedback helps the listener gain a better understanding; using "I" statements is an effective way for the speaker to express feelings.

What words do my paintings speak to people? Do they "speak a thousand words"?

Music is a universal language because: it has seven main notes, can reach the deepest parts of the human heart and soul, and can express any kind of feeling.

Storytelling is a valuable tool for teaching "lessons" to children providing the "lessons" relate to the child's world.

NOTES TO MYSELF

I am becoming more aware of how I communicate with my body and facial expressions.

Enunciate!

Read and practice using new vocabulary words.

Improve my Spanish vocabulary.

Learn how to sing some popular folk songs in their native languages.

FACILITATOR NOTES

4. Information

Preparation
> Collect Advertisement samples. Find a magazine advertisement (e.g., toothpaste, food product, athletic shoes, toy, vacation) for each student and glue onto paper. Laminate for repeated use.

Materials
Advertisement samples, two small bowls, sieve, small handful of pebbles

Presentation
INTRODUCTION—Invite students to explore Information, an aspect related to our MENTAL SELF. Ask students what they know or think they know about Information.

a. Discuss where information comes from (e.g., parents, teachers, television, books, friends, Internet, intuition). Information from various origins is quite accessible with steadily emerging technology.

b. Explore how we are constantly receiving information from what is going on around us, and what we are attracting into our lives. This information can give us valuable insight into how our own "computer minds" are operating.

c. Explore how we acquire information through our different senses. Discuss our preferred individual styles for learning and processing accumulated facts.

d. Explore how to use discernment (i.e., to come to know or recognize mentally), in regard to the information we receive. It is important to seek information from many sources and then follow what feels "right" to us.

e. Demonstrate an analogy: Take two bowls, one empty and another half filled with water. Put the pebbles into the bowl with the water. The pebbles represent other people's beliefs. Pour the water through a sieve into the empty bowl. The sieve collects the pebbles. The clear water now represents your own truth.

f. Discuss why we must be aware of false advertising and propaganda.

g. Explore how people are manipulated by brainwashing. Explore why a person might be swayed to follow a certain ideology.

h. Discuss the positive aspects of the Internet and important guidelines to follow for its usage.

i. Pass out an Advertisement sample to each student. Have them describe their feelings about the product. Discuss how the information in the advertisement works to help sell the product to consumers. Ask the students to discern if the product truly warrants their attention.

CLOSING—Ask students to comment. What questions do they have about Information? Questions can be written on their SELF-INQUIRY PAGE for exploration and research.

SELF-INQUIRY PAGE

What words would my friends use to describe me to others?

What computer skills would I like to learn?

What information would be important before relocating to a new town?

What information do people want before considering my professional services?

Why is it important to use discretion when speaking from one's heart?

4. Information

CREATIVE ACTIVITIES

1. Listen to Internet excerpts from advertisers (e.g., infomercial, political speech, movie trailer, college recruitment commercial). Which advertisements did you find compelling? How did your body feel? How would you use discernment regarding what you experienced? (Materials: computer Internet, or you can use brochures, pamphlets, television, and magazines)

2. Research and compile information about a fun outdoor activity that you would like to try in the future. Is there any information you need concerning safety? (Materials: paper, pencil)

3. What are your career aspirations? Make a list of the information you would need to consider a job of your dreams. What skills do you already possess that would be an asset for a position of employment now? Write a letter to your "employer" explaining why you would be an excellent candidate. (Materials: paper, pencil)

4. Tune in to the information your body is telling you when you first meet someone (e.g., new student, neighbor, relative). Do you feel pleased or uneasy? Explore if your body feels comfortable, or is giving you a warning to stay away. Think about someone you now know well and reflect on your initial feelings of when you first met. Do some journaling about your experiences. (Materials: journal, pen)

5. Design an attractive travel poster for a place you would like to visit. Do some research on your destination. What information can you convey about the area by pictures and words? (Materials: drawing paper, pencil, ruler, colored pencils, markers)

Information –cont.

Sample illustration by the Author: Activity 5.

Additional Ideas for Exploration
- Re-organize your backpack, notebooks, and/or desk.
- Practice using discernment while reading a newspaper or magazine.
- Look at reproductions of famous historical paintings or artifacts. Explore the information that is communicated.
- Write a report about a topic that you have picked from a "topic suggestion basket." Use many resources to gather information. Share your report with the group.
- Educate yourself on current ideas for taking care of children. (Upper grades)

MY KNOWLEDGE PAGE
(INFORMATION, DISCOVERIES, AND QUESTIONS)

The daily news from television and radio can be inaccurate or distorted, often focusing on negativity and drama.

Learning to trust my intuition will give me important insight about myself, and help me make good choices for my well-being.

Much information that we received from our early childhood became our "truth" (what our teachers told us, parents and community believed, etc.). Our mature minds have been programmed by this information we experienced. We can learn how to discard information that is no longer true for us.

Advertisers aim to convince consumers that they need their product (electronic media, brand-named clothing, job, breakfast cereal, cosmetics, etc.) to feel better or more attractive.

I would like to learn more about computer graphic design.

Name **Author**

Section **Mental**   Lesson **4 – Information**

NOTES TO MYSELF

Look deeper for accurate information not often readily available to the general public.

Don't believe everything you hear or see!

Give loving advice only when asked, and then offer it with the loving intention of helping someone.

Study quantum physics.

Put myself in the shoes of someone seeking my services. What information would I want? Use this insight as information for marketing.

FACILITATOR NOTES

5. Memory

Preparation
> Cut white paper (4" x 6"), two pieces for each student.

Materials
Human brain illustration (Internet source), white paper, colored pencils

Presentation
INTRODUCTION—Invite students to explore Memory, an aspect related to our MENTAL SELF. Ask students what they know or think they know about Memory.

    a. Show the human brain illustration and explain where memory is stored.

    b. Explore ways to describe memory (e.g., short-term, long-term, photographic, genetic—an encoding to respond in certain ways to stimuli, cellular—occurring from this life's experiences, "past-life"—believed to be of other incarnations).

    c. Explain how we have "good" memories and "bad" memories. Everything in life has a polarity. We can choose to find the "good" in every situation to free ourselves from feeling victimized.

    d. Ask students to recall an embarrassing memory they now consider humorous.

    e. Explore "déjà vu" (already seen), (i.e., a feeling that a current event or experience has happened also in one's past). Explore what happens to our memory when we transition from this life.

    f. Ask students what random facts they would wish to remember (e.g., baseball stats, bird identification, Shakespearean sonnet).

    g. Explore ways to improve one's memory (e.g., visualization association, placing objects in the environment as a reminder, repeating back new names, method of loci-association with a place).

    h. Play a memory game together. Pass out two pieces of paper to each student. Have them make a simple drawing of a favorite animal with the adult on one paper and its offspring on the other. Mix up papers and turn them over in rows. Students take turns finding matches.

CLOSING—Ask students to comment. What questions do they have about Memory? Questions can be written on their SELF-INQUIRY PAGE for exploration and research.

SELF-INQUIRY PAGE

How can I assist students in improving their memory?

What memories do I have of feeling very appreciated?

What is my earliest memory as a young child?

Why do people experience recurring dreams?

How can I remember people's names more easily?

5. Memory

CREATIVE ACTIVITIES

1. Draw a timeline map of your life. What influential events have shaped who you are today? Indicate these on your timeline. (Materials: drawing paper, pencil, colored pencils, markers)

2. Recall a pleasant memory of a holiday tradition. What details do you recall? Draw a picture of this memory. Record this memory in your journal, describing how you felt at that time. (Materials: drawing paper, crayons, journal, pen)

3. Take a challenging memory and journal about it. Can you think of any good that was a result of this experience? Draw a picture about this goodness. (Materials: journal, pen, drawing paper, colored pencils, markers)

4. Study an ancient civilization. Imagine that you are living at that time period. Write a story describing how your day unfolds. Give details about your appearance, home, family, foods you ate, and activities you engaged in. What is interesting in your life? What is difficult? Make illustrations to go with your story. Share with your group. (Materials: paper, pencil, drawing paper, colored pencils)

5. Try out some ways to boost your memory using word-association techniques or vivid mental images. Write down a list of ten different objects to gather from the room. Have a friend do the same. Exchange lists. Allow five minutes for memorization. How many items were you able to gather within a limited timeframe? How effective was your method of memorizing? (Materials: paper, pencil)

Memory –cont.

Sample illustration by the Author: Activity 1.

Additional Ideas for Exploration
- Practice remembering a shopping list by grouping items in a creative way.
- Make a photo album about your school year.
- Research your family tree.
- Gather a special object from your childhood. Show it to a friend and share its relevance in a personal story.
- Share funny memories associated with various topics (e.g., school events, vacations, holidays, sports).

Name __Author__

Section __Mental__   Lesson __5 – Memory__

MY KNOWLEDGE PAGE
(INFORMATION, DISCOVERIES, AND QUESTIONS)

Déjà vu is a feeling that one has already experienced a certain situation, although how is unclear.

I have a fond memory of some former students surprising me with a homemade cake on my birthday.

I can learn to remember facts better by creating associations between information.

Recurring dreams which include someone I know could be a message, premonition, or someone showing me "aspects" of myself that I need to integrate and take notice of.

A working memory (retaining information and using it) is an ability linked to academic performance. Instructors can assist students with "poor" working memory by repeating information, using easy to follow steps, and simple sentences.

NOTES TO MYSELF

Create a photo memory book of special events.

Make wonderful memories today!

To remember people's names - associate an image of an outstanding characteristic that begins with the first letter of their name.

Listen to classical music such as Mozart, Bach and Beethoven. Studies show it improves memory.

Live in this NOW moment.

FACILITATOR NOTES

6. Consciousness

Preparation

> Make a Consciousness poster. Write the words, Subconscious, Conscious, and Super-conscious, on a decorative poster board.

Materials

Consciousness poster, large funnel, masking tape

Presentation

INTRODUCTION—Invite students to explore Consciousness, an aspect related to our MENTAL SELF. Ask students what they know or think they know about Consciousness.

a. Display Consciousness poster.
b. Explore three terms that can be used to describe levels of our consciousness: conscious, subconscious, and Super-conscious.
   1. *Subconscious mind:* is in charge of our body processes such as heartbeat, digestion, elimination, etc. It stores memory and is the seat of emotion, habit, and instinct.
   2. *Conscious mind:* rules our life because it reasons and chooses.
   3. *Super-conscious mind:* is our unlimited potential.
c. Discuss how we can change our life by becoming aware of hidden beliefs/convictions that cause struggle and pain, by looking at what triggers strong reactions. (These may be the result of difficult experiences in which we can choose to release any blame or shame.) We can create new, empowering beliefs. Our mind is like a computer; the subconscious mind is the programming, and the conscious mind is the computer programmer.
d. Discuss how aspects of our subconscious contain positive potentials of life choices not made. It also is made up of potentials that are "negative" that are best kept from acting out. (The collective subconscious of humanity has many aspects of hatred, fear, deception, and chaos. Each human being has these to some degree in their mental programming. We can consciously disconnect from these aspects.)
e. Explore what it means to elevate one's consciousness. We can quiet our

limited thinking, and contemplate the unlimited potential of Super-consciousness that taps into universal energy. This is where one can connect to their creative genius.

   f. Demonstrate an analogy. Have a student put a piece of tape around the funnel just above the stem. The stem represents our body and the subconscious. The tape represents the conscious part of our mind. Explain how the large cone represents our mind's potential (Super-conscious).

   g. Practice visualizing a positive self-image. Have students "set" a positive, confident image of themselves in their mind. This becomes your reality as it is nourished and given attention.

CLOSING—Ask students to comment. What questions do they have about Consciousness? Questions can be written on their SELF-INQUIRY PAGE for exploration and research.

SELF-INQUIRY PAGE

Why is it important to explore my hidden beliefs?

What is the super-conscious aware of?

What about the consciousness of plants, minerals, water, and animals?

How well do I understand my purpose in life?

What is the difference between self-consciousness and a conscious awareness?

6. Consciousness

CREATIVE ACTIVITIES

1. What do you feel self-conscious about? Journal about why you feel this way. What do you really believe about yourself? What new belief are you ready to claim? (Materials: journal, pen)

2. Write three pages in your journal in a stream of consciousness without lifting your pen. What underlying theme has emerged? (Materials: journal, pen)

3. Quiet your mind and take a couple deep breaths. Close your eyes and experience a guided imagery. (Example: Meeting a guide with a gift.) *"Sitting on rock in meadow... path in distance...walk toward it...notice smells and sounds...down path and uphill ...come to garden...notice what you see and feel...birds are singing...see a fountain...and a cottage...on door is a note...your name on it...says, Please come in! Signed, Your Guide...go in...sit at table...candle burning...feels comfortable...hear footsteps...in walks guide...sits down...smiles...look closely at your guide...relax and ask a question...listen for response...sit quietly... your guide hands you a gift...thank guide...wave good-bye...follow path...through garden... see meadow...and rock...sit down."* What did you learn? Draw a picture of your gift. What does it mean to you? (Materials: recorded (optional) guided imagery, drawing paper, crayons)

4. Investigate the energy characteristics of gems and semi-precious stones. Pick a stone from a mineral collection or book, and research information about its holistic attributes. Why are you drawn to that particular mineral now? (Materials: small mineral samples or book on minerals, book on the healing qualities of gems and minerals)

5. Pair off with a partner. Take one minute to share with each other what you would like to change or improve about yourself. Take another minute to say what you like about yourself as you are. Which was easier to talk about? (Materials: none)

Consciousness –cont.

Sample illustration by the Author: Activity 3.

Golden Beads!

Additional Ideas for Exploration

- Reflect on beliefs you held when you were younger that you no longer carry.
- Be very conscious of what you think and say to others today.
- Do some journal writing about any inspiring ideas you have had lately.
- Explore dreamwork. Make an intention to remember your dreams. Write them down in first person present time. Consider what your dreams are revealing to you.
- Become more aware of how nature communicates with you.

MY KNOWLEDGE PAGE
(INFORMATION, DISCOVERIES, AND QUESTIONS)

It is by uncovering subconscious beliefs that no longer serve us that we release suffering, remove energetic blockages from our body, and permit higher consciousness to unfold.

"The deeper the pain, the bigger the receptacle for joy." Rumi

Minerals exist at the first level of consciousness.

Self-consciousness = an acute sense of self-awareness or preoccupation with oneself. Conscious awareness = a philosophical self-awareness of oneself as an individualized being.

In order to elevate our consciousness we must free ourselves from fear, ignorance, hatred, negativity, . . . and limited beliefs.

Name _Author_

Section _Mental_   Lesson _6 – Consciousness_

<u>NOTES TO MYSELF</u>

I will make an intention today to be more
conscious of my thoughts, words, and deeds.

Start a mineral collection.

I give myself permission to shine!

Communicate with nature.

Share art therapy tools for self-discovery with
other therapists.

FACILITATOR NOTES

7. Thought

Preparation
> Make Affirmation cards. Cut white cardstock paper to business card size (2" x 3"), one card for each student. Write positive affirmations on each card beginning with "I am…" (e.g., beautiful, capable of following my dreams, loved, making better choices, smart).

Materials
Affirmation cards

Presentation
INTRODUCTION—Invite students to explore Thought, an aspect related to our MENTAL SELF. Ask students what they know or think they know about Thought.

    a. Explain how our thoughts are powerful energy vibrations that "create" our lives. It is important to become aware of what we think because we attract the likeness of our thoughts back to us, whether it is positive or "negative." Likewise, our thoughts affect the physical body and its presence in the world.

    b. Discuss how our thoughts about people affect them on an energetic level. Our thought energy radiates and is received by others even if they are not conscious of it. Imagine how positive, loving thoughts can contribute to the well-being of other people.

    c. Discuss why it is important to become aware of what we truly think and believe about ourselves. When we are conscious of our core beliefs, we can release those that no longer serve us and create a new reality. It is by doing this "inner work" that we change our lives and the world around us.

    d. Explore what we are affirming in our lives by thoughts that restrict us (e.g., victim consciousness, feeling not good enough, thinking it is too late). Thought patterns can be limiting to our health, wealth, or happiness. We are in charge of our own thoughts and emotions. We have the capacity to completely eliminate negative patterns of thinking that cloud the essential nature of our mind—which is pure.

    e. Explain how "tapping" (EFT- emotional freedom technique), can significantly help to release deep-seated trauma and anxiety.

f. Discuss affirmation and visualization techniques that can promote self-confidence. *Affirmations* help to reprogram the subconscious mind with positive statements. *Visualization* techniques imprint the conscious mind with positive "pictures."

g. Lay out the Affirmation cards. Have each student pick a card and read it aloud three times, "I am ____." The group responds by repeating back, "You are ____."

CLOSING—Ask students to comment. What questions do they have about Thought? Questions can be written on their SELF-INQUIRY PAGE for exploration and research.

SELF-INQUIRY PAGE

Who or what have I harmed recently with my thoughts, words, or actions?

What beliefs about myself am I ready to let go of because they no longer serve me?

Are thoughts I am having contributing to dreams I hold for myself?

What is my philosophy of life?

What am I now "thinking" into existence?

7. Thought

CREATIVE ACTIVITIES

1. Make your own affirmation cards that can assist you at this time. Start with "I am . . ." Where will you display them to view them often? Practice visualization as you say them aloud. (Materials: index cards, markers)

2. Journal about your core beliefs. What beliefs contribute to a positive self-image? What beliefs self-sabotage or prevent you from leading a more fulfilling life? When did you first start believing this? Why? (Materials: journal, pen)

3. Think of someone you feel you harmed by your thoughts, words, or deeds. Write a letter asking them for forgiveness. (You can also still reconcile with someone who has passed on.) You need not send it, but hold the vision of being forgiven. Are you ready to forgive yourself also? Co-create a forgiveness ceremony with your friends. Make an intention to give yourself unconditional loving forgiveness. (Materials: paper, pen, materials as needed)

4. Draw a large cloud shape on a poster board. What dreams are you envisioning for yourself now? Make a dreamscape vision board by filling in your cloud with words and images. (Materials: poster board, crayons, colored pencils, markers, magazines, scissors, glue sticks)

5. Picture your life as a movie. What would be an appropriate title for this film? What genre would categorize the main plot (e.g., action, mystery, romance, comedy, fantasy)? Design an original movie poster. (Materials: drawing paper, pencil, ruler, crayons, colored pencils, markers)

Thought −cont.

Sample illustration by the Author: Activity 4.

Additional Ideas for Exploration
- Write down five thoughts that make you feel happy right now.
- Share some "food for thought" with your group.
- Practice positive magnetism. Focus on what you want, not what you don't want.
- Think "outside the box." Expand your beliefs to include something different, or that you never would have considered a possibility.
- Believe it and you can achieve it.

MY KNOWLEDGE PAGE
(INFORMATION, DISCOVERIES, AND QUESTIONS)

To change your life, change your thoughts. Expect the best.

I attract what I believe and focus my attention on.

The mind must be cleared of "negative" thinking to enjoy good health (mind-body connection).

Activity visualization - Picture yourself in positiveness or being a "winner."

I used to think that I was "not good enough." The universe reflected experiences that reinforced this belief to me until I changed my thinking.

Name _Author_

Section _Mental_   Lesson _7 - Thought_

NOTES TO MYSELF

FEEL...think...FEEL...think...FEEL

Explore EFT (Emotional Freedom Techniques).

I no longer need to wear masks. I can be genuine and authentic.

Think positive.

"The purpose of education is not to produce mere scholars, technicians, and job hunters, but integrated men and women who are free of fear; for only between such human beings can there be lasting peace." — Jiddhu Krishnumurti

FACILITATOR NOTES

8. Choice

Preparation

> Make a Choice poster. Draw an "X" at the top of a poster board. Draw a number of paths leading to the "X" beginning from the bottom of the board. Make one path straight. Make all the others meandering, or with turns and detours. Write the words, I Can Choose, on the poster.

Materials

Choice poster, classic board games of choice (e.g., chess, checkers)

Presentation

INTRODUCTION—Invite students to explore Choice, an aspect related to our MENTAL SELF. Ask students what they know or think they know about Choice.

   a. Display Choice poster. Ask students to comment.
   b. Acknowledge the many choices students have made just today. Discuss how choices we make every day impact us (e.g., how we relate to others, what we eat, movies, music, study habits). Discuss the benefits of positive choices for our energy bodies.
   c. Explain how many of the choices that we make are the result of our current perspectives. We make the best choices by increasing our knowledge and awareness.
   d. Discuss how there are really no "bad" choices in that they all provide an opportunity to learn and acquire wisdom. We can therefore let go of self-judgment. There is always a new choice we can make.
   e. Discuss how the wisest choices create more harmony in our lives. It is by changing influencing thought patterns that are fear-based that we become better able to choose wisely.
   f. Practice visualization techniques (which tap into our intuition), that can assist us in giving hints to answering questions and make choices.

   Visualization 1: *Sit in a quiet state and allow your visual screen to be blank. Ask your question, letting images form in your mind as they do in a dream. These images may be psychological aspects that you must derive meaning from.*

Visualization 2: *Imagine a gauge on your visual screen from 0 to 10. Pose a question. Let your intuition allow the gauge to fall and give you an answer.*

g. Explore how wise choices can serve our greatest good, and the good of all. Wise choices often require much courage and faith.
h. Offer the classic board games for the students to play together.

CLOSING—Ask students to comment. What questions do they have about Choice? Questions can be written on their SELF-INQUIRY PAGE for exploration and research.

SELF-INQUIRY PAGE

What am I choosing to "feed" myself (food, media, thoughts, etc.) that sustains me?

What do I procrastinate about?

How are my thoughts and choices contributing toward financial prosperity?

What will help me to make the best choices for myself?

How does society limit freedom of choice?

8. Choice

CREATIVE ACTIVITIES

1. Use a mind-map to help with a decision. A. Select a problem or subject to be mind mapped (e.g., college choice). In the center of a piece of paper, draw a circle with an image inside to represent your topic. B. Draw branches extending from your topic. Write the main aspects that are related on these lines (e.g., major, financial aid, location, size). C. Draw thinner lines off the branches. Write information related to the main aspects (e.g., astronomy, scholarships, within driving distance, large university). D. Use highlighters and arrows to make connections, emphasizing important considerations. Do you need several mind-maps to compare facts? (Materials: drawing paper, markers, highlighter markers)

2. Make a list of everyday choices that create safety for yourself and others. Have a group discussion about the dire consequences resulting from behaviors such as dishonesty, distracted driving, bullying, etc. Write down the best choices you made this week in your journal. Write about any choices that felt difficult. Why? (Materials: journal, pen)

3. What are the most urgent problems facing the world today? What are some solutions to these problems? Design a poster with a friend. Draw a vertical line to divide your poster evenly. On one side illustrate a "problem," and on the other side show how you might contribute toward a solution. Share with the group. Discuss how community organizing can be an effective action for creating positive change. (Materials: poster board, pencil, ruler, crayons, markers)

4. Journal about opportunities or dreams that you dismissed because you felt fearful. Make a painting of any fear you are harboring inside you. How large is it? Create a ritual and destroy your image if you are ready to let go of this fear. Journal about how you are becoming more confident. (Materials: journal, pen, heavyweight paper, tempera paints, brushes, rags, water container)

5. Think of a great choice you made that led to feelings of joy or opportunity. Draw an image of this. Is that choice still having an impact on your life now? Spend some time journaling. (Materials: drawing paper, crayons, colored pencils, journal, pen)

Choice – cont.

Sample illustration by the Author: Activity 5.

Move to Northern California

Additional Ideas for Exploration
- Pull one card from any picture deck and journal what it reveals to you.
- Create a "bucket list" of things you would like to do in your lifetime.
- Draw a picture of a special friend. Journal why you have chosen this person to be a part of your life now.
- Imagine owning your ideal pet. Draw an image and give your pet a name.
- Choose to be happy. It is not dependent on anything.

MY KNOWLEDGE PAGE
(INFORMATION, DISCOVERIES, AND QUESTIONS)

Many people choose fear over love, and security over growth.

Trusting my intuition and being patient, will help me make better choices.

Moving to the West Coast was a good choice for me.

Groups of people throughout history have been marginalized from society and their rights violated – children, women, Jews, Native Americans, gypsies, African Americans, LGBT, the elderly, etc. This social disadvantage crosses such disciplines as economics, politics, and education.

I used to make unhealthy choices in personal relationships that reflected a lack of self-confidence.

Name _Author_

Section _Mental_   Lesson _8 - Choice_

NOTES TO MYSELF

Be cognizant of what "energy" I ingest with my body throughout the day..

I accept responsibility for all my choices. I can always make a new choice.

I choose to be a healing agent in the world.

I choose to claim my own magnificence and mirror this for other people to see in themselves.

Give children opportunities to make their own safe choices.

FACILITATOR NOTES

9. Wisdom

Preparation
> Acquire tales of wisdom in book form or on Computer Internet.

Materials
Wisdom tales

Presentation
INTRODUCTION—Invite students to explore Wisdom, an aspect related to our MENTAL SELF. Ask students what they think they know about Wisdom.

a. Explore the meaning of wisdom. Wisdom is the antidote to ignorance (a lack of mental evolvement).

b. Discuss how wisdom is key to the future of humanity. We live in a growing technological world where wisdom will be of utmost importance for making choices that affect us all.

c. Explore the attributes of people who are "filled with wisdom." A wise person makes choices and takes action based on what is true and feels "right," and serves the greater good of all things. Everyone has the ability to acquire wisdom by taking the knowledge gained from experiences and applying them to one's life. We gain insight from challenges by changing our perspective of negativity to a positive mental outcome.

d. Discuss how living things such as the Earth, animals, and plants, are endowed with wisdom. Explore how the wisdom of nature impacts us. We can tap into the wisdom of nature by quieting our minds. This will allow us to tune in with our inner hearing to its gentle messages.

e. Discuss how all humans have an innate inner wisdom. Humility is an important character trait to develop that coincides with wisdom. A humble person will realize that they don't have all the answers, and seek counsel from a trusted source when faced with a tough decision.

f. Invite students to share a story about someone whose wisdom they respect.

g. Explore the timeless wisdom encapsulated in stories from around the world. Read a Wisdom tale and discuss its meaning.

CLOSING—Ask students to comment. What questions do they have about Wisdom? Questions can be written on their SELF-INQUIRY PAGE for exploration and research.

Name **Author**

Section **Mental** Lesson **9 – Wisdom**

SELF-INQUIRY PAGE

Whose wisdom inspires me?

What experiences in my life have provided me the opportunity to glean the greatest wisdom?

How can herbal wisdom assist me now?

What wisdom have I learned from working with children?

If I were a book...what words of wisdom would people read from me?

9. Wisdom

CREATIVE ACTIVITIES

1. Read about the life of a person considered by many people to have gifted humanity with great wisdom. Why has this person's wisdom been so revered? Write in your journal. (Materials: biography books, journal, pen)

2. Explore plant wisdom. Make a chart of some native plants. Study and record their unique qualities and healing properties. What factors enable them to thrive? Which do you find attractive? (Materials: books on healing plants, paper, pencil, ruler)

3. Think of an experience that was challenging for you. Did you garner some wisdom from this experience? Dress up as your "inner mystic" and present a discourse to friends about this learning opportunity. (Materials: materials as needed)

4. Interview an elder from your family or community. Have them share about their life adventure. What words of wisdom do they have? Draw an image that comes to mind from this meeting. (Materials: paper, pen, drawing paper, crayons)

5. Study the golden nuggets of wisdom in ancient mythology. What characters and stories do you find most fascinating? Why? Read a classic myth and write how you felt about it. Share your responses with friends. (Materials: books of mythology, paper, pencil)

Wisdom –cont.

Sample illustration by the Author: Activity 4.

Additional Ideas for Exploration
- Act out an Aesop Fable with friends and discuss the moral.
- Compile a booklet with your friends of favorite wise sayings and inspirational quotes.
- Write a song or poem that offers wisdom to others.
- Peruse the self-help/self-improvement section of your local bookstore. (Upper grades)
- Chat with your group about an inspiring television program or film you have seen.

Name __Author__

Section __Mental__   Lesson __9 – Wisdom__

MY KNOWLEDGE PAGE
(INFORMATION, DISCOVERIES, AND QUESTIONS)

Children have taught me to be playful and spontaneous. I have also grown to understand that it is important to follow their lead as to what they are ready to learn.

It is imperative in this age of rapid technological advances to view wisdom as society's precious commodity.

I learned how to be more humble, compassionate, trusting, and appreciative of life by experiencing serious health challenges.

"Darkness cannot drive out darkness; only light can do that. Hate cannot drive out hate; only love can do that." – Dr. Martin Luther King, Jr.

Golden Rule – "Do unto others, as you would have others do unto you."

NOTES TO MYSELF

Take a class on herbal lore.

I choose to live my own life and not be concerned with what others may think.

Approach life with childlike wonder and spontaneous joy!

Study the ancient, hidden wisdom that was maintained by inner groups of major cultures and handed down from generation to generation.

"We hold these truths to be self-evident that all men are created equal, that they are endowed by their Creator with certain unalienable rights, that among these are Life, Liberty, and the pursuit of Happiness." – Declaration of Independence

FACILITATOR NOTES

10. Ideas

Preparation

> Prepare Found Object bags. Provide a small, recycled, paper bag for each group of four students. Put the same random found objects in each bag (e.g., tape, string, paper clips, foam ball, pipe cleaners, cork, paper cup, straw, coffee filter).

Materials

Found Object bags for student groups

Presentation

INTRODUCTION—Invite students to explore Ideas, an aspect related to our MENTAL SELF. Ask students what they know or think they know about Ideas.

a. Explain how ideas are conceptual plans of action that use the imagination. Ideas can become dreams that we act upon.

b. Discuss some great ideas that have positively influenced how we live (e.g., electricity, telephones, computers, automobiles, airplanes).

c. Explore how great inventions can have a "negative" effect on society (e.g., automobiles and gas consumption, technology and pollution, television and misinformation).

d. Ask students to think "BIG." Discuss ideas for creating a future that is sustaining and life enhancing for all.

e. Discuss how we can take an idea and use our imagination to embellish it. Have a student suggest an idea that might improve participation in school- sponsored social events. Encourage all the students to build upon this idea with their own suggestions.

f. Explore the meaning of the expression: "thinking outside the box."

g. Divide students into small groups of four. Give each group a Found Object bag. Have them imagine and then create a unique product utilizing just what is in the bag. Share the results by encouraging each group to present a commercial for their "product."

CLOSING—Ask students to comment. What questions do they have about Ideas? Questions can be written on their SELF-INQUIRY PAGE for exploration and research.

SELF-INQUIRY PAGE

What human inventions do I appreciate most?

Whose educational philosophies do I admire?

Who would I invite to dinner if I could pick anyone?

What have I created that has benefited other people?

What does my wildest imagination wish to create?

10. Ideas

CREATIVE ACTIVITIES

1. Draw an innovative design for a means of transportation. What is it powered by? Are the materials for it sustainable? (Materials: drawing paper, pencil, ruler, crayons, colored pencils, markers)

2. Get together with your group and come up with ideas for a fundraiser. What ideas will cost the least to implement? Plan your fundraiser and give the proceeds to a local charity. (Materials: paper, pencil, materials as needed)

3. Imagine that you can go back in time and spend the day with an historical figure. Who would you pick...an inventor, teacher, writer, athlete, president, astronaut? What questions would you like to ask? In what ways are you similar? What are some of your own ideas that you would share? Draw a picture of yourself and this person. (Materials: paper, pencil, drawing paper, crayons)

4. Make friends and share ideas with global neighbors. Initiate an exchange of artwork, letters, videos, etc., with another school/learning community. What do you have in common? Organize a creative presentation of your exchange mail with other students. (Materials: materials as needed)

5. Participate in a community festival. In what ways can you help people connect with each other and nature? Make an action plan for your ideas. (Materials: paper, pencil, materials as needed)

Ideas –cont.

Sample illustration by the Author: Activity 1.

Additional Ideas for Exploration

- Create a board game to play with friends.
- Form a think tank with your group. Think of ideas to share at a student/ administrator meeting at your school.
- Invent an imaginary new product that helps people with an everyday task.
- Plan ideas for a party. Decide on a theme, decorations, music, favors, games, food, etc.
- Re- invent yourself by adopting a new "style" just for fun.

MY KNOWLEDGE PAGE
(INFORMATION, DISCOVERIES, AND QUESTIONS)

Aluminum "trees" with branches that contain solar cell-panels are now replacing streetlights.

For brain-storming (which is finding creative solutions to a problem):
Left-brain thinkers = organize ideas well using a writing format of a topic, sub-topics, and bullets.
Right-brain thinkers = organize ideas best by using mind maps; filling a paper with random thoughts which empty the mind, and then connecting related ideas with colored circles and lines.

I really appreciate telephone and airplane travel that enable me to connect easily with loved ones living at a distance.

I would love to have dinner and share ideas concerning education with the U.S. president.

Innovative building design that uses technology to reduce environmental impact supports a sustainable lifestyle, and reflects a connection with nature.

Name __Author__

Section __Mental__   Lesson __10 - Ideas__

NOTES TO MYSELF

In my wildest imagination I would create a "fantastical" treehouse!

Holistic educators have the right idea about a student's "whole person" needs: physical, mental, emotional, and spiritual.

Make a sketchbook of ideas for new creative projects.

Spend time with children, and provide them with experiences that stimulate their imagination.

Think of fun ideas for a family vacation or get-together.

FACILITATOR NOTES

Section III:
The EMOTIONAL SELF

The EMOTIONAL SELF

ENERGY/The Emotional Body/CREATIVITY

Our emotional self is our feeling nature. The emotional body holds the energetic properties that derive from the heart center. Let's explore the Emotional Self and its related aspects through the creative process.

Here are some FACTS about our EMOTIONAL SELF:
- We are responsible for our own feelings and can choose our emotions.
- Suppressed emotion harbored in our body can manifest as "dis–ease."
- Tears are healing because they remove toxicity.
- Exploring why we "react" instead of respond to experiences allows us to heal parts of ourself.
- We are more than just our bodies, minds, and emotions.
- The personal ego is our "false self," and not who we really are.
- Love is the greatest healing agent.
- Adrenalin is a secretion from the adrenal glands that affects many organs, and may contribute to the quality of our emotions.
- We cannot love others if we do not first love ourselves.
- There are no "bad" feelings.

The Emotional Self

1. Emotion
2. Expression
3. Personality
4. Healing
5. Relationships
6. Intuition
7. Empowerment
8. Compassion
9. Love
10. Freedom

1. Emotion

Preparation

> Create an Emotion collage. Glue magazine/Internet images of people expressing a range of emotions on a poster board.

> Make Feeling cards. Write a feeling word on an index card for each group member.

Materials

Emotion collage, white board, dry erase marker, Feeling cards

Presentation

INTRODUCTION—Invite students to explore Emotion, an aspect related to our EMOTIONAL SELF. Ask students what they know or think they know about Emotion.

    a. Discuss the ways people emote as a result of strong feelings (e.g., laughing, crying, shouting, smiling).

    b. Explore kinds of feelings that we experience. Have students name feeling words and list them on the board (e.g., glad, frustrated, sad, anxious, relieved). Ask students to give examples of feeling words using similes (e.g., as lonely as when a friend moves away, as exciting as opening a birthday present).

    c. Display Emotion collage. Have students guess the feeling for the different facial expressions. (Note a person may cry when happy, or laugh when nervous.)

    d. Discuss how all feelings need to be honored. Uncomfortable or painful feelings indicate what we need to heal. Denied "negative" feelings are held in our body. These buried feelings may be projected onto other people or can lead to the manifestation of physical disease. What we resist persists. We can work through the pain to feel peaceful and clear "toxins" from the body.

    e. Explain the symptoms of depression. Serious depression is dangerous in that it lowers our life force with intense feelings of hopelessness and grief. A person experiencing debilitating sadness can often be lifted from this state by getting in touch with underlying feelings of anger (a higher frequency).

f. Discuss ways to navigate through challenging feelings. It is sometimes necessary to seek professional assistance to move through strong feelings fully and in a safe way.

g. Explore how anger and fear can be beneficial. Expressing anger over an injustice can serve to create changes for the good. Fear can be a positive agent that acts as a warning signal when we are in danger.

h. Explain how smiling and being happy is a chosen response.

i. Invite students to take turns picking a Feeling card without showing it to others. Ask students to take turns "making a face" that relates to their card, while the group guesses the feeling.

j. Spend a few minutes laughing together. It is contagious!

CLOSING—Ask students to comment. What questions do they have about Emotion? Questions can be written on their SELF-INQUIRY PAGE for exploration and research.

Name _Author_

Section _Emotional_   Lesson _1 – Emotion_

SELF-INQUIRY PAGE

What events have elicited a strong reaction from me lately?

Am I harboring sadness, anger, or guilt?

What is my "emotional intelligence" now?

Why has it always been difficult for me to express anger?

Why do some people struggle with shyness?

1. Emotion

CREATIVE ACTIVITIES

1. Draw a circle on a piece of paper and divide it into eight wedges. Label each section to represent different facets of life (e.g., family, friends, school, health, leisure activities, jobs/career, faith, community interests). Write down words that describe how you feel about these areas of your life. What areas are presently unfulfilling or challenging? What beliefs do you have related to these areas? Journal why you feel the way you do. Can you make changes to have a new experience? (Materials: drawing paper, colored pencils, markers, journal, pen)

2. Write in your journal about the emotions that you are able to express freely. What is an emotion that you rarely exhibit? Why? Use clay to create a face that conveys an exaggerated expression of that emotion. Dialogue with this form in your journal. Share with a friend as a silent witness. (Materials: modeling clay, journal, pen)

3. Explore a human rights issue that you feel strongly about. Anger can be a positive force to create change in dysfuctional conditions. What action can your strong convictions serve in this cause? Do some journal writing. (Materials: journal, pen)

4. Name that tune! Think of a song that "speaks" to you lately because it stirs up personal feelings. Do you want to live in this feeling or "change your tune"? Draw an image that the song conjures up in your mind. (Materials: drawing paper, pencil, crayons, colored pencils)

5. What are you laughing about? Laughter has proven to be an effective way to boost the immune system and lighten one's sense of well-being. What would happen if you smiled more often? Create a Comedy Hour with a group of friends and entertain an audience with jokes, funny skits, etc. (Materials: materials as needed)

Emotion –cont.

Sample illustration by the Author: Activity 4.

"And I think I loved you before I met you."

Additional Ideas for Exploration
- Check in with your feelings often. Validate them all.
- Create a colorful expressive mask. Use only assorted paper, scissors, and glue. Dialogue with your group.
- Make a kinetic portrait of your family by posing friends to represent members. Do some journaling about what this "picture" reveals to you.
- Write down any personal struggles or challenges that you are ready to let go of. Shred the paper and "release" these feelings.
- Learn about Bach Flower remedies (made from spring water infused with healing flower essences, developed by Dr. Edward Bach) for reducing the negative impact of strong feelings.

Name <u>Author</u>

Section <u>Emotional</u>   Lesson <u>1 – Emotion</u>

<u>MY KNOWLEDGE PAGE</u>
(INFORMATION, DISCOVERIES, AND QUESTIONS)

Shyness (social phobia) stems from a deeply rooted fear of not being accepted by others. People can be born with a propensity towards shyness which they can work to overcome.

Joy is our natural state.

I used to believe expressing anger was a sign of weakness, feeling that it showed a lack of control. I now understand that feelings are just feelings – there are no "bad" feelings. Unexpressed anger can contribute towards dis-ease. I can seek help from a professional therapist to move through intense feelings.

It is important to consider what changes I can choose when I am feeling stressed. Long term stress can have a "negative" impact on my health.

Pervasive low energetic feelings of sadness can be lifted by laughing, watching comedy films or TV, reading books of humor, etc. – in addition to getting support from friends or a professional counselor. New studies indicate a healthy diet which includes probiotics (yogurt) can improve depression.

Name _Author_

Section _Emotional_   Lesson ___1 – Emotion___

NOTES TO MYSELF

Laugh often!

My anger needs to be channeled in a safe way, and can sometimes be a catalyst for social change.

Smile from the heart. It feels good and brightens the mood of people around me.

The emotions that people exhibit do not always match their true feelings.

It is important to validate all of my feelings and not push them away.

FACILITATOR NOTES

2. Expression

Preparation

> Create a Creative Expression collage. Glue magazine/Internet images showing ways people creatively express themselves (e.g., dancing, cooking, parenting, acting, singing, playing) on a poster board.

Materials

Creative Expression collage, paper, pencils

Presentation

INTRODUCTION—Invite students to explore Expression, an aspect related to our EMOTIONAL SELF. Ask students what they know or think they know about Expression.

a. Explore how people have expressed themselves throughout history (e.g., fashion, dance, fine art, music, literature, inventions). We have an understanding of how a culture generally felt by studying their creative artifacts.

b. Discuss how we each express our own individuality (e.g., clothing style, musical preferences, room décor, body mannerisms).

c. Display Creative Expression collage. Explain how our need for expression is the natural byproduct of our creative nature.

d. Explore how every individual is unique with personal gifts and skills to share. We can creatively express ourselves in ways that have a positive impact on others the more we get in touch with our own inner peace, joy, and passions.

e. Discuss how a negative expression of violence has impacted our world through many creative outlets. We can always choose what music we listen to, movies we watch, etc. that serve us best.

f. Imagine ways creativity might be expressed in the future. Have students write or draw on a piece of paper something wondrous that people might experience in twenty years. Encourage students to share their visions.

CLOSING—Ask students to comment. What questions do they have about Expression? Questions can be written on their SELF-INQUIRY PAGE for exploration and research.

SELF-INQUIRY PAGE

What part of me do I want to express more openly? What holds me back?

What new artistic medium would I like to try?

How can I encourage children to express themselves comfortably?

What are some things that I do well?

How am I expressing love?

2. Expression

CREATIVE ACTIVITIES

1. Gather in a small group with each person having a piece of drawing paper. Pick out appropriate words and pictures from magazines that remind you of each person. Glue these on their paper. Look at the images on your own paper. How are you seen by others? (Materials: drawing paper, magazines, scissors, glue sticks)

2. Create a group dance. First, draw together on a piece of mural paper that is placed on the floor, adding to each other's lines and shapes in the process. Begin to dance to the drawing. Let the dance evolve on its own, perhaps incorporating the paper into the movement. Allow vocal or body sounds such as clapping and stomping to emerge. Percussion instruments can be added. What felt like the dominant theme? (Materials: mural paper, markers, percussion instruments)

3. Explore the energy that you are expressing to the world most of the time. What are you attracting that is the same frequency? Think of six qualities you value most in yourself and illustrate them with a symbol. Focus on expressing these attributes more often. Write in your journal. (Materials: drawing paper, colored pencils, markers, journal, pen)

4. Journal about someone you may feel secretly envious of. What part of your "song" are they singing? Write about personal beliefs that weigh you down and prevent you from pursuing personal expression. Paint an image of how this feels. How heavy are your weights? Paint through your feelings. Continue journaling about your art process. Ask for help from the facilitator to excavate any deep issues. (Materials: heavyweight paper, tempera paints, brushes, rags, water container, journal, pen)

5. Make a self-portrait using any media. Dialogue with your completed piece in your journal. What does your portrait convey to you? (Materials: materials as needed, journal, pen)

Expression —cont.

Sample illustration by the Author: Activity 3.

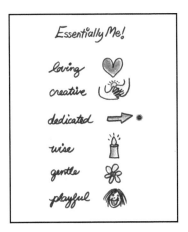

Additional Ideas for Exploration
- Study the work of a favorite artist.
- Attend a local theatre or concert performance.
- Think about what makes you feel especially joyful. Listen to up-lifting music and paint a picture of your joy.
- Design an outfit for yourself on mural paper. Outline it in proportion to your body and decorate with paint. Cut it out and tape it on!
- Enjoy playing with non-toxic face paints.

MY KNOWLEDGE PAGE
(INFORMATION, DISCOVERIES, AND QUESTIONS)

Expressive arts have no language barriers.

Art expression that dwells on the "negativity" of a social issue adversely adds energy to it by the strong focus.

It is by pursuing passionate interests and what we do well that we are able to confidently express our talents.

Every individual can choose to express their "style" in a positive way.

I can learn to be more spontaneous and freely express the fullness of life.

Name <u>*Author*</u>

Section <u>*Emotional*</u>   Lesson <u>*2 – Expression*</u>

<u>NOTES TO MYSELF</u>

Attend or listen to an opera.

Try painting with encaustics.

I create art because: I must, I can, I enjoy it, and it can be healing for myself and others.

Be me!

I will be my own cheerleader and continue expressing positive, loving messages through my art.

FACILITATOR NOTES

3. Personality

Preparation
> Acquire an assortment of hats that reflect different "personalities."

Materials
Hats, white board, dry erase marker, computer Internet

Presentation
INTRODUCTION—Invite students to explore Personality, an aspect related to our EMOTIONAL SELF. Ask students what they know or think they know about Personality.

a. Discuss the characteristics of one's personality. Certain traits describe personality (e.g., extroverted, funny, reserved, moody, bubbly, intense). Some personality theorists work at grouping personality types based on particular qualities. (A personality characteristic that can be identified in everyone is where people can be placed on an extravert-introvert scale.) Fundamental personality patterns of thoughts, feelings, and behavior make us unique; and remain fairly consistent throughout one's life.

b. Have students name and describe the personality traits of famous celebrities.

c. Explore the use of tools such as the Enneagram, personality questionnaires, astrology, etc., for gaining insight about oneself. Use the Internet to explore these topics.

d. Discuss the role of our personal ego. This is our "false" sense of self that represents how we define ourselves as reflected through the eyes of others. It distinguishes itself from other people and thrives on competition—trying to control our perception in this way. This ego does its job by serving our small self. One can consciously learn to operate from a "higher self" that is confident, yet humble, and concentrates on connecting with and serving other people.

e. Discuss how one can "build their character" beyond what can be described as the personality. Write traits on the board (e.g., honesty, humility, patience, self-control, kindness). Invite students to think of who they can look to for modeling these qualities.

f. Invite students to pick a hat. Encourage each student to "strike a pose."

Try on different hats and share how they "feel."

CLOSING—Ask students to comment. What questions do they have about Personality? Questions can be written on their SELF-INQUIRY PAGE for exploration and research.

Name _Author_

Section _Emotional_   Lesson _3 – Personality_

<u>SELF-INQUIRY PAGE</u>

What does my enneagram profile tell me about my emotional needs?

What have I believed about the ego that no longer feels true for me?

How can adults help children to build character?

How has being guided by my personal ego been problematic?

What are the origins of numerology?

3. Personality

CREATIVE ACTIVITIES

1. Ask family members to describe how you were as a young child. How do you remember yourself when you were five years old? Write a story about your life as if you were five. What new insight do you have? What would your future eighty-year-old self want to say to you now? Write a letter from your eighty-year-old self to you. (Materials: paper, pencil)

2. Imagine yourself as a tree. How would you be? Close your eyes and let an image come to you. What type of environment would you like to live in (e.g., meadow, rain forest, backyard, park)? Would you be familiar looking or would you be an imaginary tree? Paint a picture of yourself as a tree. Journal about your painting beginning with the phrase, "I am a tree..." Describe your experience as a tree. What have you witnessed? (Materials: heavyweight paper, acrylic paints, brushes, rags, water container, journal, pen)

3. If you were a recipe, what would your main ingredients be? Find objects around you that metaphorically represent qualities about your personality. Arrange your objects where you like in the room (e.g., under a table, on the windowsill). (This activity can also be done outdoors.) Share with the group. List your "ingredients" on separate scraps of paper. Read them aloud and add to a pot of, "We are all in this together soup." (Materials: small pot, paper, pencil, materials as needed)

4. Draw an image that represents your "small self." Draw another image representing your "higher self." Which is bigger? Which is in control most of the time? Paint a picture of your "higher self" embracing the "small self." (Materials: paper, pencil, drawing paper, crayons, watercolor paper, watercolor set, brushes, rags, water container)

5. Gain personal insight through the system of the Enneagram (an ancient Greek system of "personality" types). How will you use this new information on your life journey? (Materials: book on the Enneagram, paper, pencil)

Personality – cont.

Sample illustration by the Author: Activity 4.

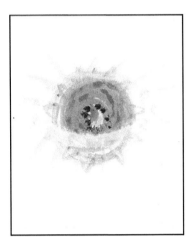

Additional Ideas for Exploration

- Don't take life too seriously. Develop a light-hearted sense of humor.
- Create a personal profile page or poster. Include photos. (Upper grades)
- Paint a picture of yourself as one of your favorite archetypal figures.
- Make an "inner dragon" puppet from found materials. Give it a voice.
- Get out of your own way!

Name *Author*

Section *Emotional*   Lesson   3 – *Personality*

MY KNOWLEDGE PAGE
(INFORMATION, DISCOVERIES, AND QUESTIONS)

The personal ego can make one feel guilty by strengthening a negative sense of identity.

Pythagoras, the great mathematician, held the belief that reality was mathematical. Origins of numerology predate Pythagoras, but he is generally considered the "father of numerology."

The psychological personal ego identifies with differences in race, gender, sexual orientation, culture, religion, politics, etc. The magnification of the personal ego increases separation consciousness and not unity consciousness.

Caregivers can help children build character by praising certain behaviors and modeling kindness, honesty, self-control, etc.

When I was growing up I attempted to build my ego to be noticed. I thought this helped me overcome feeling shy around my peers.

Name _Author_

Section _Emotional_   Lesson _3 – Personality_

<u>NOTES TO MYSELF</u>

Real empowerment comes when the personal ego is not in control.

I will align my personality with my "higher self."

I love my personality but it is not who I really am.

I identify with the Type 1-Perfectionist enneagram profile. The higher aspect of this type shows one who will work toward a goal with care, precision, and integrity.

I will get out of my own way!

FACILITATOR NOTES

4. Healing

<u>**Preparation**</u>
> Create a Healing collage. Glue magazine/Internet images that depict healing modalities (e.g., doctors, herbs, shamans, prayer, therapists, gems, color, nutrition, expressive arts, sound) on a poster board.

<u>**Materials**</u>
Healing collage, white board, dry erase marker

<u>**Presentation**</u>
INTRODUCTION—Invite students to explore Healing, an aspect related to our EMOTIONAL SELF. Ask students what they know or think they know about Healing.

    a. Discuss how humans can heal physically, mentally, emotionally, and spiritually. All domains are affected no matter where we are initially feeling the most challenged. Most physical affliction is rooted in "negative" subconscious thought patterns.

    b. Present a process for healing the mind. Write the steps on the board as you explain. 1. *Wake up.* Be attentive to your reactions, what you tend to defend, and what is showing up in your world. 2. *Embrace the feeling.* Ask yourself, "Why am I feeling this way?" 3. *Lighten the way.* Look deep within for hidden beliefs you have about yourself. 4. *Just breathe.* Breathe in and out through the mouth to activate the density, clearing it from the cellular level. 5. *Feel your love.* Quiet your mind to allow natural healing energy to sublimate "negative" patterns. 6. *Crash your hard-drive.* Re-program your mind by using active visualization and positive affirmations.

    c. Explain why it is vital to uncover how we may be holding prejudice, greed, hatred, etc. in our mind. It is important to heal these "shadow" aspects to prevent emotional behaviors being triggered when our fears arise. Fear can create an illusion of justification for judging, violating, or harming another.

    d. Explain how the healing process has many layers; certain things may take a short time to heal (a broken leg), or a longer time to heal (a "broken heart"). Often, a person can have an emotional addiction that can be difficult too overcome (e.g., being a victim, a martyr, attached to drama). A person may experience significant healing at the emotional level but not the physical.

e. Display Healing collage. Discuss the many healing approaches that assist people on a physical, mental, emotional, and spiritual level. Deep healing is an internal process that extends to the external.

f. Explain how healing is a continuous process for maintaining well-being and feeling wholeness. Our well-being positively affects the environment and people around us. When we create serenity within ourselves, we are helping to create a peaceful planet.

g. Explain how we are all healers and why love is the greatest healing force.

h. Invite the group to take turns giving each student a brief energetic healing.

One student sits in a chair and "healers" stand around the student. Healers can activate their hand chakras by extending their palms out in front of their body, one palm up and the other down. Open and close fists about twenty times. Switch palms and repeat. Healers can visualize a white protective light around their own energy body, and a grounding cord into the earth. Ask healee if he/she would like a healing before beginning (honoring their free will). Proceed if the healee replies "yes," by healers holding palms out and directing intentional loving energy. Conclude by visualizing golden suns coming down into the body through the crown of healee. Healers also do this for themselves. Healers thank the healee. (When you give a healing, you also receive a healing.)

CLOSING—Ask students to comment. What questions do they have about Healing? Questions can be written on their SELF-INQUIRY PAGE for exploration and research.

SELF-INQUIRY PAGE

Why don't some people "heal"?

How do I tactfully end relationships that I have outgrown?

Why are challenging events often the greatest opportunities for growth?

How does fine art become energetically healing for the viewer?

How are sound and music used as profound healing tools?

4. Healing

CREATIVE ACTIVITIES

1. Are you secretly addicted to unhappiness? That is your "pain-body." Draw an image of it. Use sound to allow it to express itself. Is it a loud sound? Where in your body is the sound coming from? Release this pain and allow any tears to flow. Have a facilitator witness and support your process. Write in your journal. Repeat process as needed. (Materials: drawing paper, crayons, journal, pen)

2. Explore any part of you that feels like a wounded victim. The facilitator can guide you to have a conversation with anyone by imagining the person facing you in an empty chair. Can you allow yourself to feel vulnerable? Express your feelings and how you may not condone past behavior, but are ready to begin a forgiveness process to heal yourself and move forward. Do some journal writing. (Materials: two chairs, journal, pen)

3. Paint a healing mandala to assist you in releasing any discordant energy you are ready to let go of. Incorporate the color associated with the energy centers where this emotional blockage resides. Try toning with your mandala while visually imagining a healing violet light surrounding your body. Can you congratulate yourself on the levels of healing that you are allowing to take place? (Materials: heavyweight paper, tempera paints, brushes, rags, water container)

4. What was your favorite book when you were very young? Draw a vivid picture that comes to mind. How does that book relate to your present life? Make another drawing of this connection. (Materials: drawing paper, crayons)

5. Recognize what you have recently reacted to that does not feel good. What is your hidden programming? Let your body form a gesture that exhibits this feeling. Draw a picture to express this. Are you ready to let it go? Try using breathwork and writing a positive affirmation. Share with a partner. (Materials: drawing paper, crayons)

Healing –cont.

Sample illustration by the Author: Activity 4.

HAROLD AND THE PURPLE CRAYON

Additional Ideas for Exploration

- Write a letter to your "inner child" and inquire how he/she is feeling. Answer from this part of yourself using your non-dominant hand.
- Paint a picture of how you are presently feeling.
- Get together with friends and show your baby photos. Make a promise to always take care of your "inner child."
- Make a drawing of when you felt lost. Journal about how you found your way "home" again.
- Manage feelings of stress by gently soothing yourself with calming sensory elements. (A "calming jar" can be made from a tall jar filled three quarters with water. Add one quarter clear Elmers glue and glitter. Seal top with glue.)

MY KNOWLEDGE PAGE
(INFORMATION, DISCOVERIES, AND QUESTIONS)

Real healing is the removal of blockages caused by our inner world of thought, and then reprogramming ourselves with empowering new thoughts.

Feel uncomfortable feelings, taking time to be with them but not "live" in them.

Unconditional loving forgiveness honors the fact that we all do the best we can with the knowledge we have at the time. It allows us to move forward from past hurt.

Victim consciousness is self-talk that gives us weights rather than wings.

Very challenging events in our lives cause us to stop, become introspective, and consider new choices for well-being.

NOTES TO MYSELF

Color and light in fine art can be healing by transmitting energetic frequencies to the viewer.

Respect a person's choice not to heal deep issues. Follow their lead as to how to be of assistance. Nobody can be healed from that which they are not ready to release.

Study how sound frequencies can positively aid the healing process.

Baths are healing! Hot water draws out toxins from the body to the skin's surface. As the water cools, toxins are pulled from the skin.
Basic Detox Bath: 2 cups baking soda, 1 cup Epsom salts, 1 cup sea salts, 1-2 teaspoons of glycerin (to keep skin from drying out), essential oils if desired.

Dedicate time each day for journal writing.

FACILITATOR NOTES

5. Relationships

Preparation

> Ask each participating student to bring in a photo of himself/herself with a person or animal they have a close relationship with (e.g., parent, sibling, friend, pet, coach).

Materials

Student photos, tape

Presentation

INTRODUCTION—Invite students to explore Relationships, an aspect related to our EMOTIONAL SELF. Ask students what they know or think they know about Relationships.

  a. Discuss how relationships with other people are a necessary part of human life. Interpersonal loss is the root of much human sorrow and fear. Surrounding ourselves with genuine, satisfying relationships is an important ingredient for a happy life.

  b. Explore the dynamics of different relationships (e.g., parents, siblings, friends, teachers, coaches, pets) that we encounter in our lives. We can also establish relationships with "unseen" forces such as *angels*, or *God*.

  c. Explain how all relationships help us to grow if we choose. People closest to us can be our greatest teachers. We often attract others into our life to help us heal parts of ourselves (often by "pushing our buttons"), or people that we may be able to assist. Some relationships that we establish may fall away when we have outgrown their connection and purpose. Some relationships end because a person may feel threatened by our positive change. (We may be mirroring to others who are not ready to change, perhaps having been used to getting their own needs met by unhappiness.) We cannot change anyone but can only make the best choices for our own life journey.

  d. Discuss the need to forgive others who have hurt us in any way. We can choose reconciliation by understanding that a person acts with the knowledge and wisdom available at the time, and let go. Forgiveness has many layers and is a process. Continuing to live as a victim cripples us on many levels and prevents us from experiencing a peaceful and happy life.

    e. Discuss the importance of establishing appropriate boundaries with others.

    f. Explore the "people skills" that are important to acquire and develop for healthy relationships (e.g., active listening, empathy, kindness, trust, positive regard, non-judgement, acceptance). (To resolve conflict, it is important to express feelings. Begin with, "I feel," "I felt ... when ...")

    g. Discuss how the most important relationship is with ourself. Knowing yourself and loving yourself is vital for creating a life that is a "masterpiece."

    h. Encourage each student to talk about the personal photo they brought. Display the photos.

CLOSING—Ask students to comment. What questions do they have about Relationships. Questions can be written on their SELF-INQUIRY PAGE for exploration and research.

SELF-INQUIRY PAGE

Who in my life do I accept unconditionally, love unconditionally... but can no longer be in relationship with?

Who is a "best" friend now? Why?

What things have I learned about myself from my personal relationships?

Do I unconditionally accept and love myself?

Why are birth families typically the most challenging relationships we have?

5. Relationships

CREATIVE ACTIVITIES

1. Enjoy a group dance experience. Listen to a compilation of different rhythms and styles of music that evoke certain moods. Move your body any way you feel: slow, fast, dancing with parts of your body leading, etc. Include sounds. Begin your dance alone and then mingle with other dancers by first mirroring their movements. Try connecting to a partner by sitting back-to-back, supporting and being supported by each other's movement. Continue connecting with others through movement, or perhaps move back to your own space. The group dance will evolve on its own. How did you interact with partners through movement? How did the experience feel? (Materials: technology source)

2. Draw a picture of your family. What do you notice in the picture? Who do you presently feel closest to? Are there any relationships that need repair? What can you do for yourself to heal this? What are you learning from being in this family? The facilitator will lead a group-sharing circle. (Materials: drawing paper, crayons, colored pencils, markers)

3. Who or what "pushes your buttons"? Why do you react? Seize this opportunity to embrace a part of yourself that calls to be healed. Draw an image to access deeper feelings and information. Write in your journal. (Materials: drawing paper, crayons, colored pencils, markers, journal, pen)

4. Introduce yourself to another friend by just talking about your hands. Tell your partner a story starting with "I am _____'s hands." What will they say? Describe parts of your life from the perspective of your hand's participation. Allow yourself to release any victim consciousness. Switch, and practice being the witness for your partner with positive regard. (Materials: none)

5. How is your relationship with yourself? Will you unconditionally love, honor, and cherish yourself? Create a group ceremony. Write personal vows of commitment, acknowledging aspects you want to strengthen. "I promise to love myself just the way I am," for example. Add any other effects to make your ceremony special (e.g., photos, altar, nature objects, candle, garment). Take turns reading your vows and witnessing each other. Include a symbolic keepsake to remind you of this experience. (Materials: materials as needed)

Relationships –cont.

Sample illustration by the Author: Activity 3.

Additional Ideas for Exploration

- Help organize a family folk dance party.
- Have a tea party. Talk about the qualities of friendship. Practice being an active listener. Give loving advice only if asked.
- Cultivate new friendships with people who support your learning interests and growth.
- Plan a camp-out with your group or family. Leave the electronic world behind.
- Play at a park with friends.

MY KNOWLEDGE PAGE
(INFORMATION, DISCOVERIES, AND QUESTIONS)

As people change and grow, a new identity emerges.
Friends may fall away because you may no longer
be able to relate to that person as in the past, or
you may mirror change that a friend is not ready to
make.

People who "push my buttons" are showing me
what I need to look at to heal within myself. I
have worked on how to balance giving and receiving,
develop better communication skills, and release
self-judgement...

Do I have a strong emotional support team?

Children learn much by how their parents and
guardians treat each other. They follow actions
more than words.

I am extremely grateful to be able to share life's
journey with my son and daughter.

NOTES TO MYSELF

Taking time to gaze up at the night sky helps me to contemplate my relationship with the universe.

I can still choose to be in harmony with others, even if we are in disagreement.

I teach values to children by instilling them first in myself.

I forgive me...him...her...

I am attracting meaningful relationships into my life with people of like-mind and energy.

FACILITATOR NOTES

6. Intuition

Preparation

> Make Journey signs. Cut colored poster board into shapes to represent common road signs (e.g., Stop, Go, Yield, Slow, Danger). Letter each sign with a black marker.

Materials

Journey signs

Presentation

INTRODUCTION—Invite students to explore Intuition, an aspect related to our EMOTIONAL SELF. Ask students what they know or think they know about Intuition.

a. Discuss the meaning of "using one's intuition." Everyone has the gift of intuition and can learn to trust it. Intuition is a sixth sense, an inner wisdom that is always communicating with our body and the world around us.

b. Explore how our intuition helps us. It can offer a warning signal when we are in danger, and it can guide us in maintaining good health in the body, mind, and spirit. It acts as an inner compass.

c. Have students share experiences of listening to their intuitive intelligence by trusting a "gut feeling." (When we seemed lost, we may have gotten a strong feeling of which way to turn, for example.)

d. Discuss how to discern from the chattering mind and clear, loving inner knowing.

e. Explore how one can strengthen innate intuitive abilities—natural potentialities of human intelligence (e.g., clairvoyance (clear seeing), clairaudience (clear hearing), clairsentience (clear feeling).

f. Discuss ways that we can enhance our intuition. Meditation can stimulate intuitive ability by permitting higher energies to come into the body, deepening one's awareness. Intuition is also enhanced by a positive attitude, taking care of our body, listening to the body, etc.

g. Practice intuition exercises.

Exercise 1. *Have students pair up. Take turns asking what number each other is thinking of between 1 and 15.*

Exercise 2. *Have a student hold a Journey sign behind another student's back. Student "guesses" what they feel the sign might read.*

CLOSING—Ask students to comment. What questions do they have about Intuition? Questions can be written on their SELF-INQUIRY PAGE for exploration and research.

SELF-INQUIRY PAGE

What does my intuition tell me about my personal relationships?

What can I do to develop my intuition?

Do I always listen to my own intuition...or someone else's?

How can I learn to trust myself more?

Why is it important to support the development of intuition in children?

6. Intuition

CREATIVE ACTIVITIES

1. Research some ways to enhance your intuition. What exercises help determine if you are more clairvoyant, clairaudient, or clairsentient? Practice some exercises with a friend. Be patient for your intuition to become stronger. (Materials: book on developing intuition, paper, pencil)

2. When was the last time you experienced a strong intuitive nudge? Were you contemplating a big decision? How did it feel? What action did you take? Journal about the ways intuition has guided you in the past. How is your intuition speaking to you now? Be still and listen. (Materials: journal, pen)

3. Look at your face in a mirror. Look very closely as if it is the first time you are really "seeing" yourself. Pretend you are an outside observer. Look into your eyes. What do you feel? What does that face convey to you? Write in your journal. (Materials: mirror, journal, pen)

4. Draw an image of your sixth energy center (third eye). Relax your mind and let an image form. What information does your drawing offer to you? (Materials: drawing paper, crayons, colored pencils)

5. Act out a recent dream you have had with your group by playing all the parts yourself (gestalt). Which part of the dream is the most dynamic? Encourage your friends to ask you questions so you may gain a deeper understanding of its contents. (Materials: props as needed)

Intuition –cont.

Sample illustration by the Author: Activity 4.

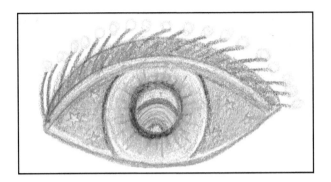

Additional Ideas for Exploration
- Practice guessing throughout the day: the time, who will come through the door, next song on the radio, etc.
- Record recurring daydreams (reveries).
- Observe animals and notice how they sense the world around them.
- Stop, find your still point inside, and listen...before you make that next big choice.
- Make a list of talents you want to further develop. Ask friends for feedback.

Name __Author__

Section __Emotional__   Lesson __6 - Intuition__

MY KNOWLEDGE PAGE
(INFORMATION, DISCOVERIES, AND QUESTIONS)

Our intuition can alert us of danger, and assist us with problem solving.

It is important to trust our own intuition and not defer to others. We each have our own inner guidance for health and better judgment.

Some children are highly intuitive. They may be empathic and feel the needs of others, or offer insights and predictions about events. They need to be supported with love and a positive attitude.

One's intuition will develop and become stronger when it is ready.

"The intuitive mind is a sacred gift and the rational mind is a faithful servant. We have created a society that honors the servant and has forgotten the gift." — Albert Einstein

NOTES TO MYSELF

Pay attention!

Keep a dream journal near the bed.

I will take care of my body and appreciate it. I will listen to the messages it provides me.

Write down intuitive hunches. Review at a later date.

Practice intuitive listening and "guessing" exercises.

FACILITATOR NOTES

7. Empowerment

Preparation

> Create a Paper crown. (A store-bought crown can be substituted.) Design and cut a crown from colored construction paper. Allow a length to fit the average head size of participating students. Decorate with markers, glitter, etc.
> Cut paper sentence strips. Allow a strip of paper for each student.

Materials

Paper crown, paper strips, pencils

Presentation

INTRODUCTION—Invite students to explore Empowerment, an aspect related to our EMOTIONAL SELF. Ask students what they know or think they know about Empowerment.

a. Explain the difference between personal empowerment and building the ego. True empowerment is a natural sense of well-being and confidence, fortified by an understanding of one's authentic self. It is a feeling of self- esteem that arises as one becomes aware of capabilities that can benefit others. Building the personal ego serves the individual self only. It is attached to improving self-image primarily to gain the appreciation of others.

b. Discuss how we all give our "power" away at times. We may give our power to friends, politicians, teachers, corporations, and substances such as alcohol, drugs, etc.

c. Explore the reasons for giving away personal power. Our power, for example, is often given to other people that we compare ourselves to when we are not in touch with our own strengths.

d. Encourage students to think about who or what they would like to take their power back from. Taking one's power back is often a process requiring small steps to realize fully.

e. Put on the Paper crown. Explain how our natural state is that of empowerment. We become a mirror to other people assisting them in recognizing their own empowerment when we claim our own "authority."

f. Have students take a strip of paper and write down a specific "strength" in which they will now claim their empowerment. Some examples might be: "I am equal to everyone..."; "I am taking responsibility for my own choices..."; "I am able to say "no" when it is appropriate for me..."; "I am able to ask for help when I need it..."; etc.

g. Invite students to take a turn wearing the crown and state what they wrote using the phrase, "I am_____, and now claim my empowerment." Have the other students repeat back the statement together. Continue with each student.

CLOSING—Ask students to comment. What questions do they have about Empowerment? Questions can be written on their SELF-INQUIRY PAGE for exploration and research.

SELF-INQUIRY PAGE

Why did I give my power away to others so often in the past?

What have been some of my most empowering actions?

How can people feel empowered despite living in situations where natural human rights are denied?

How can children learn to feel empowered, and to take healthy and safe risks?

What empowering affirmations would assist me now?

7. Empowerment

CREATIVE ACTIVITIES

1. Who or what have you given your power away to (e.g., celebrity, teacher, guru, product)? Write in your journal. Create a ceremony with your group and share what you are now taking your power back from. (Materials: journal, pen, materials as needed)

2. Think about the qualities of someone you admire. Feel yourself owning these same positive qualities. How would your life be different if they took up permanent residency inside you? Journal about how your life would be different. Draw an image of yourself radiating with these newfound qualities. (Materials: journal, pen, drawing paper, crayons, colored pencils)

3. Create an empowerment "shield." Who is your empowered self? Paint and embellish a shield shape cut from cardboard. Use powerful symbols to represent your strengths. Perhaps include a motto and symbol to honor your ancestry. Gather in a circle with your group and introduce yourself with your art. Consider incorporating sound and movement. Decorate yourself with face-paint if you like. (Materials: cardboard, construction paper, white glue, hot glue gun, hot glue sticks, masking tape, scissors, stapler, crayons, markers, acrylic paints, brushes, rags, water container, assorted craft decorations, face paint)

4. Do you suffer from "I can't-itis" in any part of your life? What is holding you back? Are you concerned that you won't do something perfect, well, or just right? Can you allow yourself to make "mistakes" and keep going? Say goodbye to your censor. Would you rather have an imperfect something or a perfect nothing? Your empowered confident self says, "I can." Find ways to say, "I can," and adopt a winning attitude. Do some journal writing. (Materials: journal, pen)

5. Make a plan for a long-term goal in your life. What smaller goals must you first attain to reach your ultimate goal? Write down the steps you need to take. Draw a map for yourself. (Materials: paper, pencil, colored pencils, markers)

Empowerment –cont.

Sample illustration by the Author: Activity 2

Additional Ideas for Exploration
- Recognize your magnificence! You are unique and valuable. Express to each member of your group what you appreciate about them.
- Chant empowering statements in a musical improvisation with friends.
- Write your own autobiographical superhero story. Tell about amazing feats you have performed, accomplishments, and what you're proud of.
- Post messages with empowering new truths on your bathroom mirror.
- Get a positive attitude adjustment.

MY KNOWLEDGE PAGE
(INFORMATION, DISCOVERIES, AND QUESTIONS)

Empowerment comes through knowing one's true identity.

I gave my power away in the past because I lacked self-esteem, and an understanding of my true nature.

Adults can teach children empowerment by being role models with positive attitudes who take positive action. Children learn through our example of making "good" choices to work through challenges.

Empowered men and women in my life act as mirrors for me.

I am confident and strong.

Name _Author_

Section _Emotional_ Lesson _7 – Empowerment_

NOTES TO MYSELF

I empower myself and others by living authentically.

Serve with humility. Be empowered and humble.

I will not give my power away to anyone or anything.

"You may never know what results come of your actions, but if you do nothing there will be no result." – Mahatma Gandhi

I will encourage autonomy for myself and my students!

FACILITATOR NOTES

8. Compassion

Preparation
> Make Compassion cards. Acquire some famous quotes on Compassion (Internet source or books). Write them on large index cards and laminate.

Materials
Compassion cards

Presentation
INTRODUCTION—Invite students to explore Compassion, an aspect related to our EMOTIONAL SELF. Ask students what they know or think they know about Compassion.

a. Share some of the quotes written on Compassion Cards.

b. Ask students to give definitions for the words "empathy" and "sympathy." *Empathy* is an understanding of someone else's experience without necessarily agreeing. *Sympathy* is feeling loss the same way someone else feels about an experience.

c. Explain how people appreciate empathy when suffering pain or loss. A person does not need to sympathize and feel pain. Offering sympathy lowers our own energy level and strengthens feelings of victimization in others.

d. Explain how *compassion* is expressing warmth and affection toward those who are suffering by adding action with empathy. It is not about trying to "fix" someone else's problem. (For example, natural disasters become an opportunity for people to experience heart-opening compassion by helping others through service and prayer.)

e. Explore what empathic and compassionate responses may be offered to people or other living creatures in various painful scenarios (e.g., "I can see that this is very difficult for you."–empathy "Let me show you around the school since you are new here."–compassion).

f. Invite students to share their experiences of feeling sympathetic, empathic, or compassionate.

g. Discuss how we can develop compassion. We can learn to be more compassionate (and non-judgmental) by being gentle with ourselves as we move through varying degrees of painful learning in our evolvement. We can choose to reach out with compassion to people who are "acting out," giving them the same tenderness we would to a sick child.

h. Discuss how we can extend compassion to our global society. Our society becomes more compassionate when we open ourselves up to understanding the suffering of others, and connect by a common human bond that we all want to be free of pain.

i. Read the Buddhist Blessing. Practice a group loving-kindness visualization.

Buddhist Blessing:
May all beings be well and happy. May all beings be free from strife. May all beings return to love. Peace be with you forevermore.

Loving-kindness Visualization: *Begin in a comfortable position. Breathe in and out from the heart center, generating kindness and love toward oneself. Send loving-kindness to a dear friend. Send loving-kindness to someone you have difficulty with. Send loving-kindness to beings everywhere.*

CLOSING—Ask students to comment. What questions do they have about Compassion? Questions can be written on their SELF-INQUIRY PAGE for exploration and research.

SELF-INQUIRY PAGE

What life experiences have helped me to be more compassionate?

When have I been "hard" on myself?

Can I be compassionate with everyone equally?

Do I show compassion for the Earth in my daily life?

Why do I sometimes feel energetically depleted when helping others in need?

8. Compassion

CREATIVE ACTIVITIES

1. Look at photos of people in various challenging experiences. Which circumstances could you easily feel compassionate toward? Where does judgment color your responses? Why? (Materials: magazine photos)

2. Journal about how compassionate you are with yourself. Are you harboring any feelings of guilt or shame for a past action? Have you pitched a tent at "Camp Suffering"? How long will you be staying? Begin now to forgive yourself and make wise new choices. (Materials: journal, pen)

3. Volunteer at a soup kitchen, or prepare some food to deliver to shut-ins. Can you exhibit empathy rather than sympathy easily? (Materials: materials as needed)

4. Create a group community service project that assists people whose basic needs are a struggle (e.g., clothing drive, book drive, toy drive). What action can you take that will benefit your community on a regular basis? (Materials: materials as needed)

5. Design a care label for the earth. Are you honoring its needs? Make a care label for yourself. How are the labels similar in content? (Materials: index cards, colored pencils)

Compassion –cont.

Sample illustration by the Author: Activity 5.

My Care Label ☆

See me with loving eyes. Support my unique spirit. Forgive me when I stumble. Accept me even though you may not agree with my choices. Listen. Hug often. Treat gently.

Additional Ideas for Exploration

- Practice anonymous random acts of kindness.
- Offer to assist an elder in your community in some way with a visit, gardening, shopping, etc. Invite some wise elders to one of your group events.
- Spend some quality time with pets.
- Read some writings by the Dalai Lama about compassion.
- Become a mentor to a younger student.

Name <u>*Author*</u>

Section <u>*Emotional*</u>   Lesson <u>*8 – Compassion*</u>

MY KNOWLEDGE PAGE
(INFORMATION, DISCOVERIES, AND QUESTIONS)

In natural disasters people tend to unite in the spirit of humanity with open hearts of compassion, disregarding each other's differences.

A person who moves through challenging situations with grace and wisdom, can then better help others do likewise.

Mother Theresa demonstrated great compassion for others.

Cultivate empathy and compassion in children by encouraging them to respond to someone else's loss that they "get it."

Be compassionate to the Earth and all sentient beings.

NOTES TO MYSELF

Get involved in a volunteer project. Devote a few hours a month.

I am dedicated to universal fellowship and peace.

A globally sustainable society respects life, economic justice, and universal human rights.

My compassion and desire to help others can be done through tithing, prayer, gifts, funding, etc. I don't always need to give with my physical presence. I will help others when I can, and when I cannot or if it does not feel appropriate at the time... it is OK to say "No."

I will be gentle with myself.

FACILITATOR NOTES

9. Love

Preparation

> Create a Love poster. Draw a large outline of a heart on a decorative poster board.

Materials

Love poster, a recording of the Beatle's song, "All You Need Is Love," technology source, drawing paper (8" x 10"), crayons, markers

Presentation

INTRODUCTION—Invite students to explore Love, an aspect related to our EMOTIONAL SELF. Ask students what they know or think they know about Love.

a. Ask students to define the word "love" in their own words.

b. Display Love poster. Invite students to name three particular things that they feel a love for (e.g., strawberries, horses, soccer). Have the students write their responses inside the heart space.

c. Discuss how love is the natural essence from which we were created. We can express love toward others to the extent that we love ourselves. Feelings of love can be expanded to other people: in friendship, with affection for a romantic partner, or a universal connectedness (selfless, unconditional)—called agape love.

d. Invite students to identify ways that people in our lives show their love for us. Share how this makes us feel.

e. *Discuss romantic love. We attract partners to us who affirm our beliefs (conscious or unconscious) about ourselves. We sometimes "fall in love" (often unrequited love) with people who reflect qualities we admire that we do not yet see in ourselves. Discuss signs of mature love. *(Upper grades)

f. Explore how we can learn to love ourselves unconditionally, and then assist the world by emanating our loving energy on every sentient being, situation, etc.

g. Pass out paper. Ask students to draw and decorate a heart in any fashion. Place them for viewing in the center of the group. Have students share ways they can demonstrate love to family members.

h. Play the song, "All You Need Is Love." Encourage students to give themselves a hug. Have a group hug. (Touch deprivation is rampant in many societies. People often crave a simple gesture of loving care and connection.)

CLOSING—Ask students to comment. What questions do they have about Love? Questions can be written on their SELF-INQUIRY PAGE for exploration and research.

SELF-INQUIRY PAGE

What new things do I really love?

What is "true love"?

Do I have to "like" someone to "love" them unconditionally?

When have I felt unloved? Unlovable?

Is it true that "love is all there is" and "what the world needs now"?

9. Love

CREATIVE ACTIVITIES

1. What do you love? Make a collage of pictures that depict things that you love. Include some of your own color-copied photographs. How many images are of things that cannot be bought? (Materials: poster board, magazines, photos, scissors, glue sticks)

2. Write a love letter to yourself. How do I love me? Count the ways... Put all the love you can muster in your letter. Mail it to yourself. (Materials: paper, pen, markers, envelope, stamp)

3. Co-create a celebration of your global family. Select a country to represent. Perform a traditional dance, song, poem, etc. Plan an international luncheon that showcases cultural diversity. What ideas do you have that can to add to the festivities? Consider inviting family members to join in this event. (Materials: materials as needed)

4. Reflect on a loved one who has passed on. What fond memories do you have? How have they enhanced your life? Honor them with a ceremony of remembrance for having been a part of your life. Know that they are still with you. (Materials: materials as needed)

5. Make a group collage to the theme of "love." Pick a focus for the images (e.g., seasons, people, animals, food). Find pictures in magazines or color-copy photos. What other kinds of elements can you contribute to this group project besides pictures? Gift your art to someone. (Materials: canvas board (18" x 24"), magazines, photos, scissors, white glue, hot glue gun, hot glue sticks, collage materials as needed)

Love –cont.

Sample illustration by the Author: Activity 1.

Additional Ideas for Exploration
- Show your appreciation for someone with a beautiful handmade gift (e.g., poem, craft, photograph, card).
- Compliment yourself and others today. Accept any compliments you receive graciously.
- Follow your passion toward a career and it will feel like play.
- Visualize a rose between you and another person when expressing hard feelings.
- Spice-up your life! Make it a grand adventure.

<u>MY KNOWLEDGE PAGE</u>
(INFORMATION, DISCOVERIES, AND QUESTIONS)

I love telling funny stories to children and listening to them laugh.

In close relationships people show their love with respect, kind acts, gifts, etc.

Love is the greatest healing agent.

I do not have to like another person to love them unconditionally. I can love anyone unconditionally (without judgement for their actions), but can choose not to associate closely with them.

"The opposite of love is fear. Love is what we came here with. Fear is what we learned here."
— Marianne Williamson

NOTES TO MYSELF

Nurturing growing children requires letting them make "mistakes" to learn in their own way, while at the same time keeping them from harms way.

Be more conscious of how loving my energy is toward others.

It is important to balance giving and receiving. Accept gifts graciously, allowing others the opportunity to give.

An alchemical practice to ease suffering in the world is—to breathe suffering into my heart, and then breathe it out transformed.

"Here is my secret. It is very simple: It is only with the heart that one can see rightly; what is essential is invisible to the eye." — Antoine de Saint-Exupéry

FACILITATOR NOTES

10. Freedom

Preparation

> Acquire a balloon or a poster board and write the word, FREEDOM, using a permanent marker. If using a balloon, inflate it and add a string.

Materials

Universal Declaration of Human Rights (a copy or excerpts)—adopted by the United Nations General Assembly in 1948 (Internet source), balloon (or poster)

Presentation

INTRODUCTION—Invite students to explore Freedom, an aspect related to our EMOTIONAL SELF. Ask students what they know or think they know about Freedom.

a. Show balloon (or poster). Explain how we are really always free when we choose to be independent and unrestricted in our minds. Real *freedom* is an identification with truth and comes with an attitude of optimism. We can be free even if our physical bodies are restricted, or if we are marginalized from society.

b. Read portions of the Universal Declaration of Human Rights. Ask students to define "sovereignty." Consider that sovereignty also means that essentially we are truly only responsible for ourselves.

c. Explore how we can "lock ourselves up" by a pessimistic attitude or feelings of victimization. Remember our happiness quotient is internal and not dependent on outside factors.

d. Explore how real freedom is learning "response—ability" from a greater sense of awareness.

e. Discuss ways in which people and organizations are helping to protect various species in our world. (e.g., Humane Society, National Wildlife Federation, Nature Conservancy).

f. Discuss the stages of life when we obtain new "liberties" (e.g., walking, talking, going to school, graduations, driving a car, getting a job). Life offers a series of beginnings that are freeing experiences of transition.

g. Have students share with a partner how free (and peaceful) they are presently feeling in their lives.

CLOSING—Ask students to comment. What questions do they have about Freedom? Questions can be written on their SELF-INQUIRY PAGE for exploration and research.

SELF-INQUIRY PAGE

What does it mean to be truly "free"?

Who were some of the 20th century's greatest social reformers?

What makes a society "free"?

What is my conscious mind "thinking" that allows me to "feel" my freedom?

How would the world be if all of humanity felt their sovereignty?

10. Freedom

CREATIVE ACTIVITIES

1. Just say "No!" It is sometimes necessary and appropriate to say no. When have you said "yes" to something and then regretted it? What were the repercussions? Can you honor a "yes" you made out of self-preservation that was really a "no"? What are you gaining from always doing for others and overextending yourself? Write in your journal about a new truth that is surfacing from within you. Journal. (Materials: journal, pen)

2. How tolerant are you? Have a group discussion sharing your experiences of not feeling accepted by others. How do we exhibit intolerance? How can we build our own tolerance levels? (Materials: none)

3. What is your resilience factor? Journal about how strong and courageous you are feeling. Have you been able to find some "magic" in what has been a difficult situation? (Eventually, circumstances from life's difficulties may lead to amazing positive influences.) Do some journaling about this. (Materials: journal, pen)

4. Design your own Freedom flag. Include your name. What colors and symbols express your sovereignty? Display your flag proudly. (Materials: heavyweight paper (18" x 24"), acrylic paints, brushes, rags, water container)

5. Create a hat to express your liberated self! Let it symbolize what you wish to spend more time being or doing. How ecstatically free and spontaneous are you feeling? Create a festive atmosphere and have a hat parade! (Materials: materials as needed)

Freedom –cont.

Sample illustration by the Author: Activity 4.

Additional Ideas for Exploration
- Make-up a victory dance with your group.
- Co- write a group poem titled, *Freedom*. Encourage everyone to take turns composing lines.
- Honor your self-discipline, trust, and courage to claim a new identity.
- Learn more about advocacy groups for political prisoners of conscience. (Upper grades)
- Be the person you were meant to be.

MY KNOWLEDGE PAGE
(INFORMATION, DISCOVERIES, AND QUESTIONS)

Children have rights and needs that are often ignored. In education, children have the right to be able to learn what will serve the development of their true potential.

We were created in freedom and not meant to be living in "bondage."

I will make choices that feel right for me. I am responsible for myself and for following my "own drummer."

All living things have natural rights that deserve respect.

I claim my personal freedom and happiness.

NOTES TO MYSELF

Think globally. Act locally.

Seek out valuable resources for what I choose to learn more about.

Stand up in consciousness for what is morally "right." Take action for social change.

Accentuate the positive. Resist giving attention to the "negative."

The Universal Declaration of Human Rights Article 26 (2) "Education shall be directed to the full development of the human personality and to the strengthening of respect for human rights and human freedom. It shall promote understanding, tolerance, and friendship among all nations, racial, or religious groups; and shall further the activities of the United Nations for the maintenance of peace."

FACILITATOR NOTES

Section IV:
The SPIRITUAL SELF

The
SPIRITUAL
SELF

ENERGY/The Spiritual Body/CREATIVITY

Our spiritual self is connected to all of life. The spiritual body holds the "divine" essence that is our true identity. Let's explore the Spiritual Self and its related aspects through the creative process.

Here are some PRINCIPLES about our SPIRITUAL SELF:

- We are spiritual beings having a human experience.
- Spirituality reveals our true nature—love.
- Our spiritual identity informs all other aspects of the self.
- Spirituality reminds us of our connection to all life.
- Love, peace, abundance, joy, and creativity are our birthrights.
- There is One Life.
- Our spiritual body connects us to the universal source of creation.
- Enlightenment is knowing oneself.
- Spiritual materialism is a self-deception of strengthening the personal ego through spiritual techniques.
- We are co-creators with the *Creator*.

The Spiritual Self

1. Spirit
2. Soul
3. Spirituality
4. Evolvement
5. Meditation
6. Spiritual Heritage
7. Communication
8. Divine Guidance
9. Creator
10. Oneness

1. Spirit

Preparation

> Make Human Paper forms. Use a Body Outline (see template) to trace and cut six paper forms from white paper.

Materials

Human Paper forms, penlight/flashlight, song lyric sheet of Russian Christian's song, "You Gotta Sing," percussion instruments

Presentation

INTRODUCTION—Invite students to explore Spirit, an aspect related to our SPIRITUAL SELF. Ask students what they know or think they know about Spirit.

    a. Discuss how spirit is our animating principle. (An analogy would be like a puppet that comes to"life" through voice and action.) Consider our spirit to be the energy of love and goodness (or *"God"* energy) that moves through all human beings, and present in all life.

    b. Discuss how our spirit is sometimes shrouded with density—a result of fear, "negative" self-talk, personal ego identity, poor eating habits, etc.

    c. *Present the Human Paper form by holding the layers together upright. Shine a penlight at a 45° angle from the back towards the heart center. (This represents the energy of our spirit.) Demonstrate how "inner work" helps to remove density. This raises our frequency and allows love to shine brighter through us. (Remove the layers one by one to reveal the brightest light through the first form.)

    d. Discuss the pathway of meditation and self-reflection to heighten our awareness and remove "negativity."

    e. Invite students to share experiences of feeling inspired (i.e. in-spirit).

    f. Explore how we often forget that it is this energy of love moving through us that brings forth goodness. True credit for our accomplishments does not gratify the ego, but recognizes this *"inspiration"* as the real "doer.")

    g. Sing, "You Gotta Sing." Invite students to sing together, taking turns substituting inspiring words (e.g., love, give, play, hug) for,"You gotta

*Directive adapted from the book, *Honoring the Light of the Child (2004)*, by Sonnie McFarland.*

_____when the spirit says _____ ..."

CLOSING—Ask students to comment. What questions do they have about Spirit? Questions can be written on their SELF-INQUIRY PAGE for exploration and research.

Name _Author_

Section _Spiritual_ Lesson _1 – Spirit_

<u>SELF-INQUIRY PAGE</u>

When have I felt a lack of "Spirit"?

Do I feel inspired in my career choice?

What do the spiritual qualities of animals offer to humans?

How is my spirit today?

What constitutes a spiritual awakening?

1. Spirit

CREATIVE ACTIVITIES

1. When has "the Spirit moved you"? Describe the experience in a painting. What was the circumstance? How did it feel? (Materials: heavyweight paper, tempera paints, brushes, rags, water container)

2. Draw a mind-map to explore how you can develop your talents or pursue your interests. What resources are available? Is there a leadership role you feel inspired to take? Create a plan of action. Do some journaling about this. (Materials: drawing paper, colored pencils, journal, pen)

3. Experience a visualization of a golden source of universal energy coming through your crown energy center, clearing and energizing you. How do you feel? Draw an image of this. Hang it in your room to remind you to repeat this visualization often. (Materials: drawing paper, crayons)

4. What qualities do animals have that also live inside of you? Use clay to create an imaginary animal having combined characteristics of animals you identify with (e.g., body of a lion, tail of a dog, head of an eagle). Write about your creation and how it is like yourself. "I am courageous like a lion, devoted like a dog, perceptive like an eagle ..." (Materials: modeling clay, paper, pencil)

5. Who has mirrored unconditional love to you? What people in your life do you enjoy being with because you feel wonderful in their presence? How many people do you think would answer *you* to those questions? Write in your journal. (Materials: journal, pen)

Spirit – cont.

Sample illustration by the Author: Activity 1.

Additional Ideas for Exploration

- Try being enthusiastic about everything today. Journal about your day before going to sleep.
- Sing "This Little Light of Mine."
- Visit an aquarium or petting zoo.
- Have a sacred fire ceremony with your group if permitted. Ignite your zest for embracing life!
- Use the arts to process intense feelings for a cathartic experience.

Name __Author__

Section __Spiritual__   Lesson __1 - Spirit__

MY KNOWLEDGE PAGE
(INFORMATION, DISCOVERIES, AND QUESTIONS)

A spiritual awakening is an unfold-ment of awareness — recognizing the divine in ourselves, and in the world around us.

"Kundalini" is our inherent spiritual power.

The clarity and quality of our divine expression is dependent on our degree of conscious awareness.

I feel inspired and passionate about my career choices. Opportunities flow easily on my path now.

It is when I am tired or feel stressful that my connection to Spirit becomes clouded. I can help myself by meditating and having positive thoughts.

Name *Author*

Section *Spiritual*   Lesson   *1 – Spirit*

NOTES TO MYSELF

I am never alone.

People tend to remember not what you did, but how you made them feel.

Let the Spirit move me!

Spirit is loving energy that imbues all life.

Do what you love and "work" will follow.

FACILITATOR NOTES

2. Soul

<u>**Preparation**</u>

> Make Soul Portrait samples. Glue front-facing portrait photos of people and animals onto cardstock paper. Laminate for repeated use. (Color-copy photos first.)

<u>**Materials**</u>

Soul Portrait samples

<u>**Presentation**</u>

INTRODUCTION—Invite students to explore the Soul, an aspect related to our SPIRITUAL SELF. Ask students what they know or think they know about the Soul.

    a. Explore the meaning of soul as the eternal, spiritual essence embodied in each of us as human beings. Our soul works harmoniously with the physical body, mind, and emotions for each individual's highest good and the highest good of all.

    b. Discuss how as individual souls in human form, there is a purpose for each of our lives.

    c. Discuss the nature of soul groups—souls who have similar life missions (e.g., healers, teachers, messengers, system busters).

    d. Discuss the concept of mineral, plant, and animal kingdoms having an over-lighting group soul.

    e. Explore reincarnation and the evolvement of souls. (It can be understood that there is no death as a soul continues to evolve after passing from this plane to a new life. The form may change, but our substance does not. As spiritual beings, we choose to incarnate on a physical plane to learn and evolve.)

    f. Display Soul Portrait samples. Sense the sacred connection of all life by looking closely at the faces. Notice the eyes as "windows to the soul."

    g. Have students silently meander around the room looking into each other's eyes. Invite them to acknowledge their spiritual connection with everyone they pass by.

CLOSING—Ask students to comment. What questions do they have about the Soul? Questions can be written on their SELF-INQUIRY PAGE for exploration and research.

Name <u>Author</u>

Section <u>Spiritual</u>   Lesson <u>2 – Soul</u>

SELF-INQUIRY PAGE

Does my soul travel?

How does my soul evolve?

Do I have more than one soulmate?

What is my soul group?

What living things have souls besides humans?

2. Soul

CREATIVE ACTIVITIES

1. Get centered and conjure an image that represents your soul. What are the unique qualities that it contains? Describe your soul in your journal. (Materials: drawing paper, crayons, colored pencils, journal, pen)

2. Would you like to take a pilgrimage? There are thousands of sacred sites on the planet. Research some of these places that you would like to visit. Plan a pilgrimage to one sacred site. Gather photos and information about your destination. Journal about what you hope to attain from your journey. "Create" a map from your home to this site. Use your imagination to feel yourself embarking on your pilgrimage. Visualize yourself connecting to the energy and people there. Draw an image of this trip. Record the experience in your journal. (Materials: books on sacred sites, drawing paper, crayons, colored pencils, journal, pen)

3. Journal about the lessons you have learned from your birth family. Why do you think you "chose" your relatives? The people closest to us can be our greatest teachers. Do some journaling about any recent self-discoveries. (Materials: journal, pen)

4. Create a soul collage titled, *My Heart and Soul.* Paint on canvas board and glue pictures, words, fabric, beads, etc., to express the theme. Does your piece reflect your own special touch? Embellish it in any way to create a pleasing arrangement. (Materials: canvas board (11" x 14"), acrylic paints, brushes, rags, water container, photos, magazines, scissors, white glue, hot glue gun, hot glue sticks, craft decorations, collage materials as needed)

5. Make up a story of your own creation. How did your soul come to be? Draw a picture to illustrate your story. (Materials: paper, pencil, drawing paper, crayons, colored pencils)

Soul –cont.

Sample illustration by the Author: Activity 1.

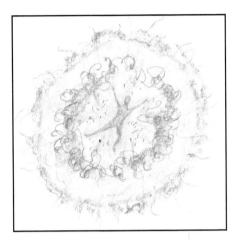

Additional Ideas for Exploration

- Practice greeting people at a soul level. Connect by seeing them with loving eyes and as your equal.
- Become a pen pal with a student from another school; or a wise elder from a local senior center.
- Explore beliefs concerning reincarnation.
- Spend some quality time with preschool children. Honor their big spirits in little bodies.
- Listen to some "soul" music, while you enjoy some "soul" food with friends.

MY KNOWLEDGE PAGE
(INFORMATION, DISCOVERIES, AND QUESTIONS)

My soul is forever gaining wisdom and evolving.

Three kingdoms have group souls: animals, plants, and minerals.

A soulmate can be defined as anyone we have a spiritual agreement with, have a lesson to learn from, or whom we have agreed to teach in order to release karma.

The soul is eternal, infinite, and limitless.

I would like to make a spiritual pilgrimage to Peru and see Machu Picchu.

NOTES TO MYSELF

Each soul has its own path to follow. I do not know what is best for another soul.

Respect everyone as a "soulmate."

My soul is eternal.

I can take a pilgrimage to a sacred site through guided imagery.

The eyes are windows to the soul. Let love shine through.

FACILITATOR NOTES

3. Spirituality

Preparation

> Arrange floor pillows for students in a circle. (Optional) Place a lit candle in the center.

> Create Spiritual Literacy cards. Write down key words for bringing spirituality into our daily life (e.g., unity, unconditional love, gratitude, kindness, justice, beauty, devotion, peace, faith, attention, hope, connection) on index cards.

Materials

Sacred texts (e.g., Bible, Buddhist Sutras, Bhagavad Gita), Spiritual Literacy cards, floor pillows (optional), candle, matches

Presentation

INTRODUCTION—Invite students to explore Spirituality, an aspect related to our SPIRITUAL SELF. Ask students what they know or think they know about Spirituality.

a. Explain religion vs. spirituality. *Religion* is a man-made belief system about God held by a group of people, formed from the passing on of sacred teachings by legendary founders. Every chosen path to spiritual wholeness is to be honored. (However, differences in religious beliefs have been fuel for separation and conflict in human history. Some people of religion attempt to control people's lives by indoctrinating with fear and dogma.) *Spirituality* is the awareness of our natural state of oneness with all life. It is not a thing, rather an atmosphere of a universal feeling of love, truth, goodness, and beauty.

b. Display a few sacred texts. Give students an opportunity to look through the books.

c. Discuss some of the religions of the world and how they originated. Explore how people develop religious belief systems.

d. Explore common spiritual principles of the major religions (e.g., Golden Rule, brotherly love, goodness). All major religions include spiritual commitments of contemplation, prayer, service, and study.

e. Discuss how spiritual development leads one to live a meaningful life with a positive trajectory for the future. Moral values such as compassion, beauty, justice, and peace are enhanced. (A spiritual worldview can lead to humanity treating each other as friends.)

f. Ask students if they are open to exploring their spirituality. A commitment to follow a spiritual path requires a willingness to work on the self to become more aware, and remember one's true nature. This "inner work" becomes our spiritual practice. It is an ongoing process that can be arduous and challenging, but leads to great fulfillment and peace of mind.

g. Place the Spiritual Literacy cards in the center of the circle. Invite students to share what the words mean to them.

CLOSING—Ask students to comment. What questions do they have about Spirituality? Questions can be written on their SELF-INQUIRY PAGE for exploration and research.

Name <u>Author</u>

Section <u>Spiritual</u>   Lesson <u>3 – Spirituality</u>

<u>SELF-INQUIRY PAGE</u>

<u>What are some historic facts regarding the</u>
<u>formation of the major religions?</u>

<u>How was the Goddess (divine feminine) revered in</u>
<u>various cultures throughout history?</u>

<u>What were some of the spiritual beliefs held by</u>
<u>people of ancient Egypt?</u>

<u>What are some common spiritual beliefs of</u>
<u>indigenous people?</u>

<u>How has an understanding of my spiritual nature</u>
<u>made my life more meaningful?</u>

3. Spirituality

CREATIVE ACTIVITIES

1. Take a walk in nature. Commune with the life forces around you and receive their nourishment. Breathe in the energy of the sun, sky, trees, water, etc. These natural elements surround us and are a part of us. Can you feel how you are connected to all of life? (Materials: none)

2. What is your spiritual practice? Does it need to be revised? Write down a format for a daily practice that you can follow easily (e.g., prayer, meditation, energy tools, affirmations, intentions, blessings, dreamwork, visioning, journaling, gratitude list). (Materials: paper, pencil)

3. Create a drumming circle with your group using themes for inspiration (e.g., celebration, unity, elements of nature). Consider making a drum from a found object. Can you drum to the earth? (Materials: drums of various kinds)

4. Paint an image that describes an "ah-ha" moment (peak experience). How are you different now as a result? (Materials: heavyweight paper, tempera paints, brushes, rags, water container)

5. Write a personal review/response for a book you have read on spirituality. What books are "calling" to you now? Share your review with your group. (Materials: books on spirituality, paper, pencil)

Spirituality – cont.

Sample illustration by the Author: Activity 4.

Additional Ideas for Exploration

- Explore the spiritual practices and beliefs of indigenous people.
- Spend part of a day in silent retreat.
- Establish a "community" of spiritual support with your friends.
- Lighten up by giving away anything you no longer need. Share with others in the group.
- Commune with an object of nature. Create an expressive art piece such as a poem, dance, or painting about your experience.

MY KNOWLEDGE PAGE
(INFORMATION, DISCOVERIES, AND QUESTIONS)

The idea that spiritual forces exist in the natural world (clouds, animals, wind, etc.) is a common theme in Native American traditions. Different tribes have developed their own creation stories, heroes, and deities.

"New Age" philosophy is not really new. The teachings are ancient, but what is new is the greatest shift in consciousness happening on this planet.

Life never ends. We transition from this life to a new expression of existence. There is never separation from loved ones.

We are born from love, live in love, and will eventually return to love.

My understanding is that the "job" of us humans is to awaken to our true nature, enjoy life, and manifest our gifts to help others. The benefits of this are: peace, joy, and abundance; which will then extend outward and be felt by all life forms.

NOTES TO MYSELF

"When one tugs at a single thing in nature, one finds it is attached to the rest of the world."
– John Muir

I am a spiritual being having a human experience.

"As educators our goal is not so much the imparting of knowledge, as the unveiling and developing of spiritual energy." – Maria Montesorri

I am so grateful for teachers and guides who light my path showing me the way.

Keep doing the inner work. It's never over!

FACILITATOR NOTES

4. Evolvement

Preparation

> Create an Instructions for Life on Earth poster. Write the words, Instructions for Life on Earth, as a top heading on a poster board. Decorate the border, leaving the middle blank.

Materials

Photo of the Earth in vast space, Instructions for Life on Earth poster, markers

Presentation

INTRODUCTION—Invite students to explore Evolvement, an aspect related to our SPIRITUAL SELF. Ask students what they know or think they know about Evolvement.

    a. Display the photo of the Earth in space. Ask students what they feel when looking at the image.

    b. Discuss how our lives here on Earth are like attending a school (Earth School), and how we learn and spiritually evolve through our human experiences. Explore how we tend to "repeat" lessons that become more difficult until we "get" it. On Earth our free will is honored as we create our own experiences.

    c. Explore what the real purposes are for our education here on Earth (e.g., acquiring wisdom, sharing our gifts, learning to live in joy, appreciation, gratitude). As a collective, learning how to bring the energies of the masculine and feminine powers into balance on this planet is a vital focus now.

    d. Discuss who the guides are in our life. These may include living people and spiritual guides not in a physical body. Guides are teachers who assist us on our life journey. (We are all teachers and students.) Explore how a teacher may also be in the form of a flower, animal, elemental, etc.

    e. Explore what "contracts" we may have for this life. Consider that we are born with spiritual contracts (i.e., learning experiences) that we have agreed to, that help us grow (evolve) and enjoy life. We make other contracts along the way of our life path by our own free will. (We can choose to nullify contracts that no longer serve us.)

f. Discuss how different cultures view death. Death frightens many people because it is an unknown, a loss of familiar "life." Ancient mystery school teachings tell us that we are "dying" all the time to old beliefs and birthing discovered truths. We transition physically to a new expression of life.

g. Explore the possibilities of life on Earth in the next decades.

h. Present Instructions for Life on Earth poster. Have students think of life "instructions" that they might have received (and "forgotten") after being born. Write them on the poster board.

CLOSING—Ask students to comment. What questions do they have about Evolvement? Questions can be written on their SELF-INQUIRY PAGE for exploration and research.

Name <u>*Author*</u>

Section <u>*Spiritual*</u> Lesson <u>4 – *Evolvement*</u>

<u>SELF-INQUIRY PAGE</u>

What have I come to share in this lifetime?

Do people repeat "grades"? Skip "grades"?

When have I felt like a failure?

What "lessons" am I working on?

How have my own children been great teachers to me?

4. Evolvement

CREATIVE ACTIVITIES

1. Journal about the subjects you are currently studying in life. Give them titles (e.g., Unconditional Love, Creating Abundance, Releasing Judgment, Compassion 101). What are you currently getting "good grades" in? (Materials: journal, pen)

2. Think of life lessons you have learned. Present a lesson that you "aced" to your group in an artistic way, by using any art modality (e.g., pictures, drama, music). Why did you need to learn this? Did you learn this lesson with difficulty or ease? Congratulate yourself. (Materials: materials as needed)

3. Study the Universal Laws (Internet source) that govern our existence (e.g., Law of Attraction, Law of Abundance, Law of Tithing, Law of Cause and Effect). Choose a Law and paint a poster to represent it. Title your painting. How well are you following this law? Write in your journal. (Materials: poster board, tempera paints, brushes, rags, water container, journal, pen)

4. Paint an abstract picture describing your feelings about death. Allow any uncomfortable feelings to emerge on the paper. Do you hold any sadness or fear? Journal with your image and then destroy it by ripping, crumpling, or cutting it up. Now, transform it into a new and beautiful creation. Add to it, or use pieces in some way to make a new form. Journal about difficult feelings, and make more space for joy. (Materials: heavyweight paper, tempera paints, brushes, rags, water container, extra materials as needed, journal, pen)

5. What life choices can you personally make to enhance and protect the planet? Make a list and a pledge. (Materials: paper, pencil)

Evolvement – cont.

Sample illustration by the Author: Activity 5.

Additional Ideas for Exploration

- Draw a picture of a garden. Label each plant with an identifying trait now growing within you.
- Do some journal writing about how you triumphed through a "dark night of the soul."
- Know that everywhere you've been was where you had to be to get to NOW!
- Write a letter to beings on a highly evolved planet. Ask them for advice in creating harmony on Earth.
- Practice "riding the waves" of life like a professional surfer.

MY KNOWLEDGE PAGE
(INFORMATION, DISCOVERIES, AND QUESTIONS)

I am balancing my masculine and feminine aspects.

Lessons we do not learn the first time are repeated, becoming more challenging.

Earth has been a very dense planet, but veils into other realms are now being lifted.

Universal Laws – There are main Laws that guide us all, such as: Law of Transmutation, Law of Attraction, Law of Cause and Effect, Law of Polarity, Law of Tithing, Law of Oneness, etc.

We are all teachers and students to each other. My children are good teachers of integrity, discernment, and playful spontaneity.

<u>NOTES TO MYSELF</u>

We can only help people as far as we have been ourselves.

I am now focused on being a businesswoman, powerful communicator, and humble co-creator with the universe.

Earth School is a place to learn, grow, and follow my dreams.

Many evolved souls are arriving on the planet to assist humanity at this time. In the last few decades children described as being "indigo" have been born, who want to change what is wrong with society that's not in integrity with higher ideals. Many of these children have been labeled as ADHD, or ADD. Young children we see now, are mostly right-brain oriented and do not fit well into traditional schooling environments that focus on linear-logical learning (left-brained orientation).

We have all chosen to be here on Earth at this time.

FACILITATOR NOTES

5. Meditation

Preparation

> Arrange floor pillows for students in a circle. (Optional)

Materials

Meditation music, technology source, bell or chime for meditation, floor pillows (optional)

Presentation

INTRODUCTION—Invite students to explore Meditation, an aspect related to our SPIRITUAL SELF. Ask students what they know or think they know about Meditation.

    a. Explain the definition of meditation. Meditation is withdrawing our mind and senses from the outside world, and turning inward to stillness.

    b. Explain the change in brain wave patterns that are a result of meditation. During a "normal" working process, the brain pulsates beta waves. During meditation, the brain shifts to alpha, and even theta waves. This helps to release stress and allows one to access expanded realms of creativity.

    c. Discuss the benefits of this practice. Meditation offers a healing and rejuvenating effect on the body. Meditating can help us to raise our consciousness and connect to divine presence within—generating great shifts in one's life perspective.

    d. Discuss ways to practice meditation (e.g., sitting in stillness with intention, walking in nature undisturbed by background noise). Meditation need not be difficult. It can easily begin as a quiet contemplation in which to achieve a sense of balance, inner peace, and wisdom.

    e. Explore ways of creating personal space for a contemplation/meditation practice. (This does not require anything fancy; can even be a pillow or chair that you will designate for this purpose.)

    f. Discuss the basics of a sitting meditation. Practice "going within."

Invite students to sit in a chair in a straight position with feet on the floor, hands comfortably on laps. Relax the body by taking a few deep breaths. Close eyes and bring your inner vision to your sixth energy center. Allow thoughts to float by... always coming back to the breath. Music may be played while the group sits for a short period. Ring chime to end meditation.

CLOSING—Ask students to comment. What questions do they have about Meditation? Questions can be written on their SELF-INQUIRY PAGE for exploration and research.

SELF-INQUIRY PAGE

How can I teach young children to practice meditation in a school setting?

What type of meditative practice can I commit to?

How has meditation helped me?

What revelations have I gained from quiet contemplation?

What are the benefits of group meditation?

5. Meditation

CREATIVE ACTIVITIES

1. Practice a walking meditation in nature paying attention to the breath with each step. What mantra feels appropriate to repeat as you walk? (Materials: none)

2. Do you have a comfortable place for meditation? Create a space in your home for daily practice. Consider a quiet area and include soft lighting, pillow, blanket, music, altar, etc. (Materials: materials as needed)

3. Have a group meditation sitting outside in a natural setting. Chant the sound of "AUM" together before you begin. (This is considered the primordial sound of creation.) What was your experience like? (Materials: bell or chime)

4. Create a painting while listening to uplifting music. How does the music make you feel? (Materials: watercolor paper, watercolor set, brushes, rags, water container, technology source)

5. Imagine that a sculpture has been created of you. It portrays your "higher" more evolved self, and is waiting for you in a studio under a covering. Go into the studio and remove the cover. What do you see? Make an illustration of your sculpture. Dialogue with your drawing in your journal. (Materials: drawing paper, colored pencils, journal, pen)

Meditation – cont.

Sample illustration by the Author: Activity 5.

Additional Ideas for Exploration

- Form a meditation group by designating a specific time that everyone will "sit" together, even though you reside in different locations.
- Learn how to take some inspirational photographs of nature.
- Create a guided imagery to share with the group.
- Locate a labyrinth in your area and take the walk.
- Make something decorative for your sacred space.

Name <u>*Author*</u>

Section <u>*Spiritual*</u>   Lesson <u>*5 – Meditation*</u>

MY KNOWLEDGE PAGE
(INFORMATION, DISCOVERIES, AND QUESTIONS)

Children can be taught how to sit "silently," and then take a few minutes to notice their breath while relaxing.

Painting, singing, and journaling can be contemplative activities for me.

There are different types of meditation such as: sitting meditation and "going within," contemplating the breath, insight meditation, walking meditation, meditation on an idea, mantra meditation.

Meditation benefits for the body include: stress reduction, pain reduction, brain activation, immune system enhancement, serotonin increase, blood pressure balance, etc.

Meditation has improved my health and ability to concentrate, influenced my artwork, and has deepened my connection to all of life.

Name _Author_

Section _Spiritual_   Lesson _5 - Meditation_

<u>NOTES TO MYSELF</u>

Practice meditating regularly with a group.

Meditate in nature often.

There is a still, quiet center within myself that I can go to no matter what is happening around me.

My daily meditation practice establishes and maintains my connection to God's presence within me to receive guidance.

Be a silent witness to the witness.

FACILITATOR NOTES

6. Spiritual Heritage

Preparation
> Make a poster. Write the words, It Is So Good, It Must Be True, on a decorative poster board.

Materials
Poster

Presentation:
INTRODUCTION—Invite students to explore Spiritual Heritage, an aspect related to our SPIRITUAL SELF. Ask students what they know or think they know about Spiritual Heritage.

a. Explore the meaning of "spiritual heritage." An understanding of spiritual heritage is that we as human beings (souls) are individualized expressions of the *Creator* with vast potentialities. (The unlimited divine self is sometimes referred to as our "*God-Self.*")

b. Explore why we do not claim our birthright of joy and freedom. People often choose to live in suffering by becoming attached to their "stories." We are not meant to suffer. Explore the expression, "It's too good to be true."

c. Discuss how unconditional loving forgiveness helps to release pain, allowing more happiness to enter our lives.

d. Explore how faith, hope, and charity can be considered the greatest attributes for humans to foster. *Faith* grounds us. It is a trusting in a relationship with the divine. *Hope* lifts us. It acts as a buoy, offering meaning to every experience despite the "outcome." *Charity* is love. Charity is brought forth and magnified when any harboring fear we are holding onto is cleared away.

e. Discuss how we don't need to "search" for anything when we can trust that there is a purpose and plan for our lives.

f. Explore what a new era on Earth will herald in. Unprecedented shifts in humanity's consciousness and the Earth are now occurring. We are all participating in a transformational planetary "ascension" process.

g. Display poster. Have students share what the words mean to them.

CLOSING—Ask students to comment. What questions do they have about Spiritual Heritage? Questions can be written on their SELF-INQUIRY PAGE for exploration and research.

Name *Author*

Section *Spiritual*   Lesson *6 – Spiritual Heritage*

SELF-INQUIRY PAGE

What does my spiritual heritage promise me?

When did I think "bad" times were coming because I didn't feel I deserved too much happiness?

What is most important for me to remember about my spiritual heritage?

Has my soul incarnated into other forms besides a human being on Earth?

What is the most amazing gift I could give myself right now?

6. Spiritual Heritage

CREATIVE ACTIVITIES

1. Paint a group mural depicting a large sun (signifying Universal energy) with radiating sunbeams. Imagine that you are a sunbeam. Feel yourself radiating from this energy. What does spirituality reveal as your true origin? Write in your journal how this perspective may change your outlook on life. (Materials: mural paper, tempera paints (many pre-mixed colors in cups with brushes), rags, water container, journal, pen)

2. Celebrate your awakening process with a "happy un-birthday" party with your group. "Gift" each other by writing a "wish" on pieces of paper for each person. What are your own wishes? (Materials: materials as needed, paper, pencils)

3. Compose a poem about "grace." When have you experienced grace in your life? (Materials: paper, pencil)

4. What holds you back from helping to create "heaven" on Earth? Who is telling you that it is not possible? Are you listening to the "small self" or your "higher self"? Do some journal writing. Create a painting titled, *Heaven on Earth*, imagining a world of beauty, harmony, and love. Start with an image of heaven, then contain it within an image of the Earth. (Materials: watercolor paper, watercolor set, brushes, rags, water container, journal, pen)

5. Read about the life of a mystic (e.g., Yogananda, Mother Theresa, Jesus, Gandhi, Gautama Buddha, Amma). What readings inspired you? Share a few favorite passages with a friend from a book you have read. (Materials: books on the lives of mystics.)

Spiritual Heritage – cont.

Sample illustration by the Author: Activity 4.

Additional Ideas for Exploration

- Draw a picture of a time capsule for future visitors from another galaxy. Make sketches of artifacts you would include in it that portray humans as very evolved beings.
- Imagine a "past life" through guided imagery. Journal about what you experienced and learned.
- Write about the spiritual principles that are guiding your life now.
- Be IN love and EN-joy!
- Allow yourself to really feel that your *Creator* loves you unconditionally. Truly.

Name _Author_

Section _Spiritual_   Lesson _6 - Spiritual Heritage_

MY KNOWLEDGE PAGE
(INFORMATION, DISCOVERIES, AND QUESTIONS)

'Autobiography of a Yogi' by Paramahansa Yogananda is a classic spiritual book that illuminates the deepest secrets of life. This continues to be an important book that introduces Eastern philosophy to the West.

Hildegard of Binen was a famous medieval artist who became a nun. She had "visions" that informed many written works, performed sacred music, and also shared a great understanding of herbal medicine.

I will claim my divine birthright. It is not dependent on my "earning" it — only by saying "yes" with conscious gratitude, and truth of identity.

Absolute freedom is above all human laws.

I could gift myself right now by taking some "time out" from studying/working to have some fun in the outdoors.

Name _Author_

Section _Spiritual_   Lesson _6 – Spiritual Heritage_

NOTES TO MYSELF

"Live Well, Laugh Often, Love Much." — Anonymous

Try past-life recall.

I say "yes" to bringing heaven on earth.

Faith, hope and charity are my guiding attributes.

Agape is a term for the spiritual love God has for mankind—that extends to a universal love of one's fellow man.

FACILITATOR NOTES

7. Communication

Preparation
> Create a Prayer collage. Glue Internet images that depict people of various spiritual practices engaged in prayer (e.g., Sufi dancers, Tibetan monks making sand mandalas, Native Americans drumming, Buddhist chanting) on a poster board.

Materials
Prayer collage

Presentation
INTRODUCTION—Invite students to explore Communication, an aspect related to our SPIRITUAL SELF. Ask students what they know or think they know about Communication.

a. Display prayer collage. Discuss the different ways people communicate to divine presence through conventional prayer or creative expression.
b. Explore the different traditions of prayerful communication.
c. Explore the power of prayer. Studies indicate that many people praying together with a specific intention manifests powerful results.
d. Discuss how we can learn to pray effectively. Effective prayer is to ask for guidance on the next step in one's life, or to acknowledge the superb perfection of another person and their life path. (Praying to ask for another person to change interferes with their personal sacred journey. Praying for "negative" circumstances to change adds to the problem by a focused attention.) Communicating with the *Creator* through prayer is to ultimately get the conscious part of our mind in alignment with divine will.
e. Explain a type of prayer called affirmative prayer. *Traditional prayer* can be based in uncertainty. *Affirmative prayer* is a prayer spoken with a feeling tone of faith and conviction that a positive outcome is already present.
f. *Describe the basic steps for a type of affirmative prayer called a *Spiritual Mind Treatment* (Steps A-E) in which one would use ones own wording.. This prayer requires that one's daily attitude agree with the prayer by guarding every thought. *(Upper grades)

* Spiritual Mind Treatment

The following is a sample prayer for self-forgiveness.

STEPS:

1. Recognition — *I acknowledge that God is all there is, an infinite light of unconditional love. All is good and all is God. There is nothing but divine perfection in all situations and all beings.*

2. Unification — *I know that I, (person's name) am one with the infinite consciousness of love and light. My soul is forever united with the perfection of all that is. I am inseparable from my Creator and the infinite flow of wisdom and creativity.*

3. Realization — *I speak my word knowing that the realization of love, peace, and truth are mine. I am the goodness that is one with my Creator. I know that all of my experiences are opportunities for me to grow and gain wisdom. I am now allowing unconditional loving forgiveness to fill my heart.*

4. Thanksgiving — *I am grateful for divine presence within me to guide my actions. I am gentle with myself knowing that I always do my best at any given time.*

5. Release — *I now release my action to the Law. I have spoken my truth and know unconditional love and forgiveness are mine now and always. I release this answered prayer, I let go and let God. So be it. So it is. Amen.* (Concluding a prayer with, "So Be It. So it is," gives it the seal of faith.)

g. Explain to students that they can communicate with divine presence in any way they choose. Encourage an attitude of faith and focused attention.

h. Have the students create a simple affirmative prayer together. Sample:

> *I trust the unfolding of this day. I am thankful for the beauty I will notice, and the perfect circumstances crossing my path for my highest good. I am filled with gratitude. So It Is.*

CLOSING—Ask students to comment. What questions do they have about Communication? Questions can be written on their SELF-INQUIRY PAGE for exploration and research.

SELF-INQUIRY PAGE

What are some of the ways that indigenous people pray?

What prayers would I like to memorize?

When have I felt alone and separated from my true essence?

What are some creative ways that I can communicate with the divine?

What is The Serenity Prayer?

7. Communication

CREATIVE ACTIVITIES

1. Pray to be shown the next step to take in your life. Embrace faith that your answer will be revealed to you in some way (e.g., movie title, book, sign, a conversation). Are you feeling more courageous, optimistic, and peaceful by a practice of daily prayer? (Materials: none)

2. Do you have a favorite prayer? Write the words to a favorite prayer on drawing paper and decorate it. Why is it special to you? (Materials: drawing paper, pencil, ruler, markers, colored pencils, rubber stamps, stamp pads)

3. Create a prayer chamber with your group for someone who has requested support. If possible, "send" your prayer with the rising smoke of incense. Can you release this prayer knowing that it has been received? (Materials: candle, incense, matches)

4. What are you grateful for? Design a gratitude prayer using words and images from magazines glued on a poster board. Think of the many little things that you can be thankful for. (Materials: poster board, magazines, scissors, glue sticks, markers, glitter)

5. Design an artistic altar display. Draw and cut out three panels from a piece of cardboard to form a triptych. Tape the seams and gesso the cardboard on both sides. Paint or draw inspiring pictures, symbols, and words. Glue photos or magazine images. Decorate your altar to make it meaningful to you. Where will you place this triptych in your home? What other significant objects will you place in your altar space? (Materials: medium-weight cardboard (11" x 14"), X-acto knife, pencil, ruler, masking tape, gesso. acrylic paints, brushes, rags, water container, magazines, photos, scissors, white glue, glue sticks, hot glue gun, hot glue sticks, collage materials as needed)

Communication –cont.

Sample illustration by the Author: Activity 4.

Additional Ideas for Exploration

- Make prayer flags. Write blessings for the Earth on strips of cloth (3" x 12"). Decorate with acrylic paints or fabric markers. Tie finished cloths to a line of string. Hang it outside for the wind to carry off your messages.
- Do a full-moon ritual. Speak your intentions for the next month into a glass of water. Add a cover and leave it outside overnight. Drink it in the morning.
- Ask for a prayer from someone else.
- At the end of each day say aloud ten things you're grateful for and how it makes you feel. Also think of something you want to manifest, saying it aloud with gratitude as if it is already true.
- Dance your prayers. Make a drawing describing how this felt.

Name __Author__

Section __Spiritual__   Lesson __7 – Communication__

MY KNOWLEDGE PAGE
(INFORMATION, DISCOVERIES, AND QUESTIONS)

Verbal prayer is one way to talk to God. I can also communicate through writing, movement, ritual, music, etc.

The words of the Lord's Prayer vibrate at a high frequency.

Prayers are received and always answered. My needs are known.

Reinhold Niebuhr wrote the Serenity Prayer in the 1930's. It was originally intended for a sermon and was not actually published until the 1950's.
"God grant me the Serenity to accept things I cannot change, Courage to change those things I can, and Wisdom to know the difference."

Indigenous people often use ritual and ceremony (incorporating expressive arts elements) centered on the theme of nature as a way of communicating with a universal power.

Name **Author**

Section **Spiritual**   Lesson **7 - Communication**

NOTES TO MYSELF

Memorize the Prayer of Saint Francis.

Read some sacred poetry.

I will try singing my prayers.

Think of things to be grateful for at the end of
each day.

Use affirmative prayer, which affirms that the
"good" is already manifested.

FACILITATOR NOTES

8. Divine Guidance

Preparation
> Cut out one body outline from cardboard (see template).
> Arrange floor pillows for students in a circle. (Optional)

Materials
One large white poster board, body outline, tape, colored markers, floor pillows (optional)

Presentation
INTRODUCTION—Invite students to explore Divine Guidance, an aspect related to our SPIRITUAL SELF. Ask students what they know or think they know about Divine Guidance.

    a. Explore the meaning of divine guidance. Divine guidance assists us on our life journey, originating from a source of pure love and intention. It can be received through quiet contemplation, and by people and things that come into our lives. This communication is always available to us.

    b. Create a visual representation of this guidance process. Have a student tape the body outline at the bottom of the poster board. This represents a human being on Earth. Invite a couple of students at a time to draw an image or write a word describing a source of divine guidance (e.g., people, books, animals, nature elements, angels) any place on the board.

    c. Discuss the many ways that we can express our spiritual awareness in daily activities (e.g., dancing, singing, conversation, assisting others, writing, playing, optimistic attitude). We become spiritual guides for others when we live our lives with loving intention.

    d. Explore our willingness to be clear channels of divine energy. It is more important how we are in the world than what we "do." It is when we are living in joy, gratitude, and appreciation that we are open to clear guidance. We then "vibrate" above the chaos and can inspire others to resonate with us.

    e. Invite students to repeat the following phrase out loud with conviction, "I am love. I am light." Have students take turns repeating to others, "You are love. You are light." Have students repeat together as a group, "We express love. We express light."

CLOSING—Ask students to comment. What questions do they have about Divine Guidance? Questions can be written on their SELF-INQUIRY PAGE for exploration and research.

SELF-INQUIRY PAGE

What powerful messages of higher wisdom will assist me on my path now?

How is automatic writing done?

What were the circumstances when I felt I was being "divinely guided"?

What is the "sacred path" in Buddhism?

How can right-brain thinking provide spiritual guidance?

8. Divine Guidance

CREATIVE ACTIVITIES

1. Journal about ways you have escaped emotional pain, or relieved feelings of emptiness (e.g., excessive computer activity, alcohol abuse, frequent shopping, overeating). Have you sought help for any addictions that are controlling you? Shine the light on thoughts you have that are causing you pain. Do some drawing to facilitate the process. (Materials: journal, pen, drawing paper, crayons)

2. How are you expressing "*GOoDness*" in your life? How has this gifted other people? Draw an image that comes to mind. Write in your journal. (Materials: drawing paper, crayons, journal, pen)

3. Imagine yourself surrounded by loving white light. In quiet contemplation, invoke the presence of one of your spiritual guides. Feel and trust their presence. What do you wish to say? How do they respond? Journal about this experience. (Materials: journal, pen)

4. Journal about a time when you felt you were at a crossroads in your life. Think of the people who influenced you positively and assisted you along your path. Who has been a significant "tour guide" in your life? (Materials: journal, pen)

5. What animals are you drawn to? Draw four "power" animals that are guiding you now, intuitively placing each one in a direction on the Medicine Wheel outline (see template). Consider this symbolic interpretation for the four directions: NORTH represents winter, a time of resting; EAST represents spring, a time of beginning; SOUTH represents summer, a time of growth; and WEST represents autumn, a time of preparation for change. What position is affecting you at this time? Read about your four animals in a book on totems and discover what the sacred wisdom/support each animal may be offering. Write about this information in your journal. (Materials: Medicine Wheel copy, crayons, colored pencils, book on animal totems, journal, pen)

Divine Guidance – cont.

Sample illustration by the Author: Activity 5.

Additional Ideas for Exploration
* Discern what guidance feels loving and true for you.
- "Invite" the presence of a favorite mystic to accompany you on a walk in nature.
- Ask for help from an *angel.* (They love to help but honor your free will, assisting only if asked.)
- Allow miracles to happen.
- Channel love into your work and daily activities.

MY KNOWLEDGE PAGE
(INFORMATION, DISCOVERIES, AND QUESTIONS)

Everyone channels divine energy through his or her own creative loving expression.

There are now many channeled messages coming through people holding a high consciousness, both vocally and in written word. This divine wisdom serves to help guide humanity at this pivotal time in history.

Artists and right-brain thinking can connect with higher realms of inspiration to create profound works of expression through dance, music, poetry, painting, etc.

I have felt divinely guided to read certain books, and connect with specific people who have opened doors for my artistic expression.

Inner wisdom is our own spiritual guidance that facilitates the connection between the soul and the embodied self. Spiritual wisdom may be distorted by inner blockages of pain that we might carry.

NOTES TO MYSELF

My daily rituals and spiritual practice are very important in establishing a "tone" for my day.

"When the student is ready, the teacher will appear." – Gautama Buddha

Learn more about Freemasonry.

All answers are within me.

I am supported in all areas of my life.

FACILITATOR NOTES

9. Creator

Preparation
> Display the Sun mural from Spiritual Lesson #6: Creative Activity 1.
> Take a smiling photo of each student. Have them printed.
> Arrange floor pillows for students in a circle. (Optional)

Materials
Sun mural, camera, student photos, colored markers, masking tape, earth globe, floor pillows (optional), candle, matches

Presentation
INTRODUCTION—Invite students to explore the Creator, an aspect related to our SPIRITUAL SELF. Ask students what they know or think they know about the Creator.

a. Explore words that signify the *Creator* (e.g., *God, Goddess, Spirit, Universal Energy, Prime Source*). This presence is known by many names.

b. Explore the knowing of the *Creator* as a divine energy of unconditional love. (Some religions portray *Creator/God* as a judgmental force whose wrath is to be feared.) Consider *Creator* to be an omnipotent, omnipresent, omniscient presence.

c. Discuss the principle of the *Creator's* energy being in all forms of life.

d. Discuss how we are powerful co-creators with the *Creator*. We are born with intelligence and individualized will to create our lives with every thought and choice. The universe supports us regardless of what we choose to affirm for ourselves. Contemplating on divine presence assists us in the direction of our life.

e. Discuss how our "homecoming" is remembering who we really are as spiritual beings.

f. Share an analogy: *Creator* is like the source of electricity, and we as human beings are the light bulbs. The electricity is always there. We can choose to turn up the dimmer switch and "lighten up." We decide the "level," and awareness. There are times when this connection catches our attention, and times when it just is.

g. Create a visual representation of the *Creator*. Direct the student's attention to the Sun mural. Invite students to tape their photos on the sun's rays. Have students draw images of other "life" forms (e.g., animals, nature elements) around the sun.

h. Have a peace meditation. Invite students to sit in a circle. Place a lit candle and earth globe in the center.

Meditation for Peace: *Close your eyes and take a few deep breaths to feel centered. Visualize yourself filled with love and peace. Extend your awareness to everyone in the room affirming the same for them. Now extend to everyone in your town/city. Continue in concentric circles to your state... country... all people on the continent...people on the entire planet and beyond. Sit for ten minutes.*

CLOSING—Ask students to comment. What questions do they have about the Creator? Questions can be written on their SELF-INQUIRY PAGE exploration and research.

Name __Author__

Section __Spiritual__   Lesson ___9 – Creator___

<u>SELF-INQUIRY PAGE</u>

How would I paint an image of Universal Energy?

How often am I aligned with my divinity in thought, word, and deed throughout my day?

What do I feel I "know"?

What is my understanding of the Creator now?

When is it most difficult for people to feel divine presence?

9. Creator

CREATIVE ACTIVITIES

1. Paint an image that reflects your ideas about the Creator. How does this image speak to you? Dialogue with your image in your journal. (Materials: heavyweight paper, acrylic paints, brushes, rags, water container, journal, pen)

2. Bless everyone you meet today silently. Bless your teachers and friends. Bless food before you eat it. Bless any money that passes through your hands and all who will touch it. How does this make you feel at the end of the day? Did you notice anything different? Write in your journal. (Materials: journal, pen)

3. Design a gratitude card to yourself. Can you feel gratitude for every experience of your life, even the most challenging? All your experiences are opportunities to learn and unfold to your truth. Be thankful for all you can right now. Wherever you are on your journey is good. (Materials: drawing paper, pencil, ruler, colored pencils, markers, rubber stamps, stamp pads)

4. Do you feel you "don't have enough"? What areas of your life do you feel lack (e.g., friends, talent, money, love, support)? Remind yourself that you are already abundant. Affirm that the divine is present in all things and positive results are in action. What action steps do you feel you can take now? Do some journaling. (Materials: journal, pen)

5. Write a sacred contract promising to love and be a humble servant on this planet through your daily activities. Make an intention to release and destroy any contracts you may be adhering to that no longer serve you. Create a sacred ritual for yourself. What can you include in your ritual that will add powerful energy (e.g., roses, candle, bowl of water, feather, stones)? Renew your vows periodically. (Upper grades) (Materials: materials as needed)

Creator –cont.

Sample illustration by the Author: Activity 1.

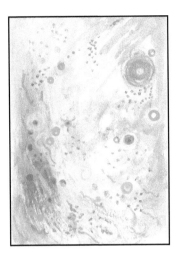

Additional Ideas for Exploration

- Give yourself permission to be "imperfectly perfect." Decorate a proclamation for yourself.
- Keep discovering new truths about yourself.
- Connect to your divine presence throughout the day. Carry something in your pocket that reminds you that you're never alone.
- Create a haiku about the beauty of nature.
- Spend some time with newborn baby beings.

Name __Author__

Section __Spiritual__   Lesson __9 – Creator__

MY KNOWLEDGE PAGE
(INFORMATION, DISCOVERIES, AND QUESTIONS)

Being in a natural setting helps one to feel a universal consciousness.

"I AM" is God's presence within me.

It is difficult to feel divine presence when one succumbs to fear. Fear can obliterate the remembrance of one's true identity.

I am dedicated to living in accordance to the Universal Laws, continuously doing my "inner-work", and having a daily practice.

I know we are all treasure troves!

Name <u>Author</u>

Section <u>Spiritual</u>   Lesson <u>9 – Creator</u>

NOTES TO MYSELF

<u>Bless everyone and everything I come in contact</u>
<u>with today.</u>

<u>God is my source and my supply.</u>

<u>I am love, loved, loving, lovable.</u>

<u>"God/Goddess" is in me and every face I see.</u>

<u>"The truth shall set you free." – Jesus</u>

FACILITATOR NOTES

10. Oneness

Preparation

> Make a Oneness circle. Draw and cut out a large circle (about 18" in diameter or larger) on a piece of heavyweight paper. Mark one side of the paper with a yellow crayon.

> Arrange floor pillows for students in a circle. (Optional)

> Display mural from Spiritual Lesson #9.

Materials

Life mural, a musical recording of John Newton's song, "Amazing Grace," technology source, Oneness circle, masking tape, crayons, colored pencils, markers, floor pillows (optional)

Presentation

INTRODUCTION—Invite students to explore Oneness, an aspect related to our SPIRITUAL SELF. Ask students what they know or think they know about Oneness.

a. Discuss Oneness. *Oneness* is unity consciousness; an understanding that there is no separation, and all life is connected. Contemplate that as human beings we are energetically connected to each other, animals, plants ... the universe ... and all that is (*Creator/Creation*). This signifies that there is really one mind, one body, one spirit ... all is One. (It could be understood that we were all born into this dense physical plane for the most part forgetting our true identity. Souls incarnating now will have a clearer remembrance of who and what they are.)

b. Explain the importance of the world now adopting a spiritual worldview. A spiritual worldview promotes global friendship and peace.

c. Explore how we are all co-creators in the art of life where miracles are the norm.

d. Show Oneness circle. Have each student cut a shape from the circle, with the facilitator taking the last piece. Ask the students to design their name in any way on the white side of the paper.

e. Play the song, "Amazing Grace." Have the students put the puzzle together fitting the pieces from the yellow side up. Tape the puzzle from the yellow back. Turn it over to reveal "oneness."

    f. Sit in a circle around the artwork. Be in silence for a few minutes holding hands (left palm up, right palm down).

    g. Encourage students to consider how their "inner work" has positively affected the entire matrix of life. Invite students to verbalize personal feelings of Oneness as a result of this group journey.

CLOSING—Ask students to comment. What questions do they have about Oneness? Questions can be written on their SELF-INQUIRY PAGE for exploration and research.

Name _Author_

Section _Spiritual_   Lesson _10 - Oneness_

SELF-INQUIRY PAGE

When has it been challenging to feel unified with all of humanity?

How can I anchor oneness more fully?

What did the great mystics teach about unity consciousness?

How can I respond to people living in "separation"?

Why are many people now becoming more spiritually conscious?

10. Oneness

CREATIVE ACTIVITIES

1. Who are you? What are you? What is your life purpose? Do some journal writing about how you walk in oneness on the planet and assist in its evolvement. (Materials: journal, pen)

2. Create sacred performance art. Collaborate with your group as you each contribute ideas to a co-creative performance. How can you express your affirmation of oneness through art media? Use costumes, props, song, prayer, etc., to share your unique interpretation. Invite friends to witness. (Materials: materials as needed)

3. What treasures have you discovered on your creative journey? Design a treasure chest with your group using a discarded shoebox. Make some "gold" coins from cut circles of cardboard painted gold. Write a special "treasure" on each coin signifying what you have acquired (e.g., tolerance, patience, faith, humility, confidence, friendship, wisdom). Personal discoveries and new truths may also be written on the coins. (Materials: shoebox, gesso, acrylic paints including gold, brushes, rags, water container, cardboard, scissors, black permanent marker, craft decorations, white glue, glitter, collage materials as needed)

4. Paint a group mural. What colors, lines, shapes, and images express your feelings about the self-discovery journey that you have all shared together? Play inspiring music and have fun! Title your piece, *Our Journey Together*. (Materials: mural paper, newspaper, tempera paints (many pre-mixed colors in cups with brushes), rags, water container, inspirational up-beat music, technology source)

5. How do you envision the next "chapter" of your life? Write a mission statement and refer to it often. (Materials: paper, pencil, colored pencils, markers)

6. Reflect on your self-discovery experience. Congratulate yourself on the work you have done for yourself that has a great ripple effect on the entire planet. This completion is your new beginning. Spend a few minutes moving freely about the room to get in touch with your body. When you feel ready, have a friend trace your body

Oneness —cont.

on mural paper. Decorate it in any way to express yourself. How have you transformed? Who is the authentic new you emerging? Spend some time journaling. Share with the group. (Materials: mural paper, pencil, crayons, colored pencils, markers, colored construction paper, scissors, white glue, collage materials as needed, journal, pen)

Sample illustration by the Author: Activity 2.

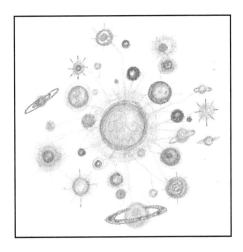

Additional Ideas for Exploration
- Practice loving everyone unconditionally in your life. Accept everyone as they are, even if you do not agree with them.
- Make homemade candles as gifts.
- Draw your name on a blank piece of paper and have a friend tape it on your back. Gather with your group and anonymously write down beautiful reflections that you have witnessed in each person. You are beautiful!
- Chant the Gayatri Mantra (Internet source).
- Remember **All-is-One!**

MY KNOWLEDGE PAGE
(INFORMATION, DISCOVERIES, AND QUESTIONS)

Oneness cannot be felt when the personal ego is allowed to be in control.

Will all religions eventually blend into one universal spiritual practice?

Love and accept everyone as they are. See every person as an equal with no judgment. We have all been in various stages of consciousness but our true identity is as One Life.

Leave seeds of wisdom for others to nurture in their own time. Be a wayshower for those people who may ask for "directions." They in turn will lead others.

When we are not "for-giving," we are in separation.

Name _Author_

Section _Spiritual_   Lesson _10 – Oneness_

NOTES TO MYSELF

Visualize peace and loving energy surrounding our
planet and all its inhabitants.

Salute the good in everything. See the highest in
everyone, but use discernement to understand where
people are "operating" from.

Today is a new beginning. I have new opportunities
for radiating love, creating peace, and gathering
wisdom.

I know that I am one with the divine energy of all
that is. I experience this amazing power as the
expression of my own being.

I am you. You are me. We are One.

FACILITATOR NOTES

Appendix

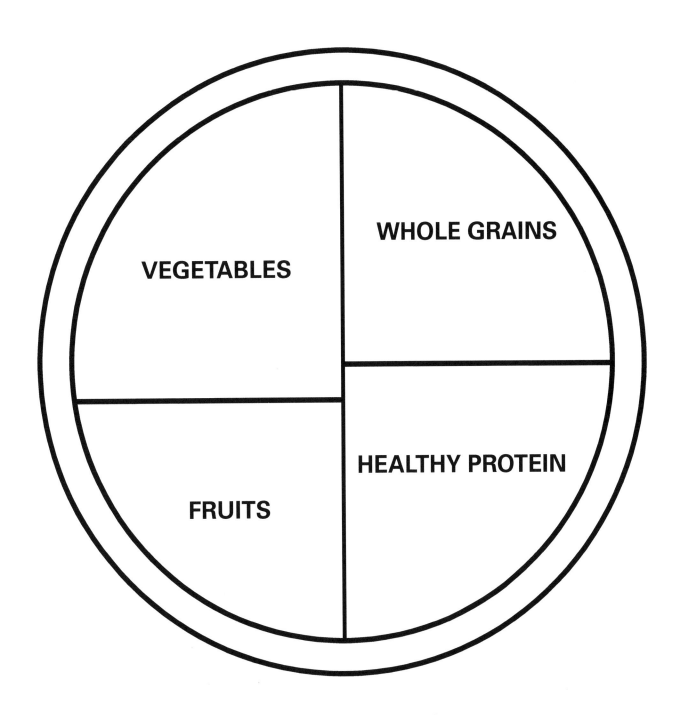

VEGETABLES

WHOLE GRAINS

FRUITS

HEALTHY PROTEIN

*Adapted from The Healthy Eating Plate—
Harvard School of Public Health, The Nutrition Source
www.hsph.harvard.edu/nutritionsource

Template a.

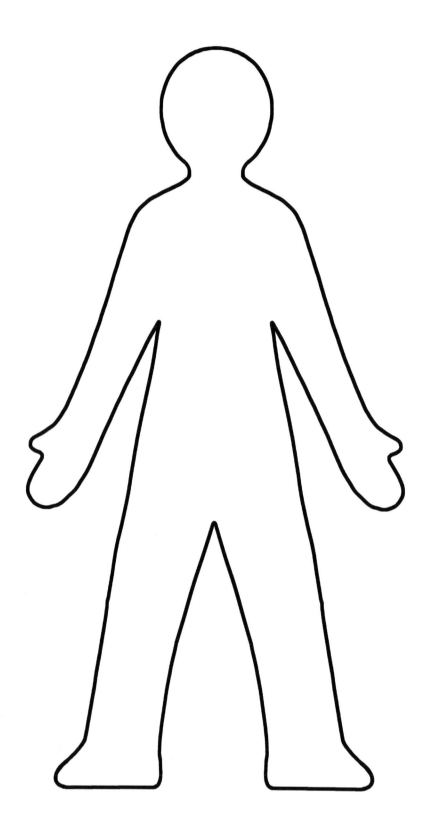

Template b.

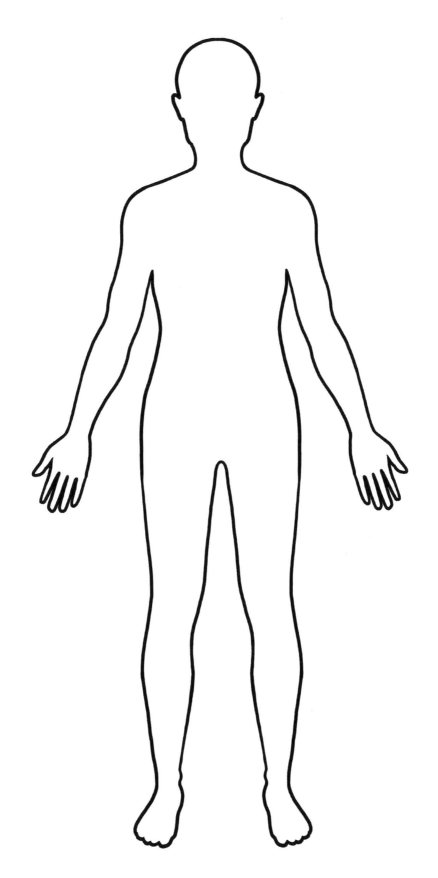

Template c.

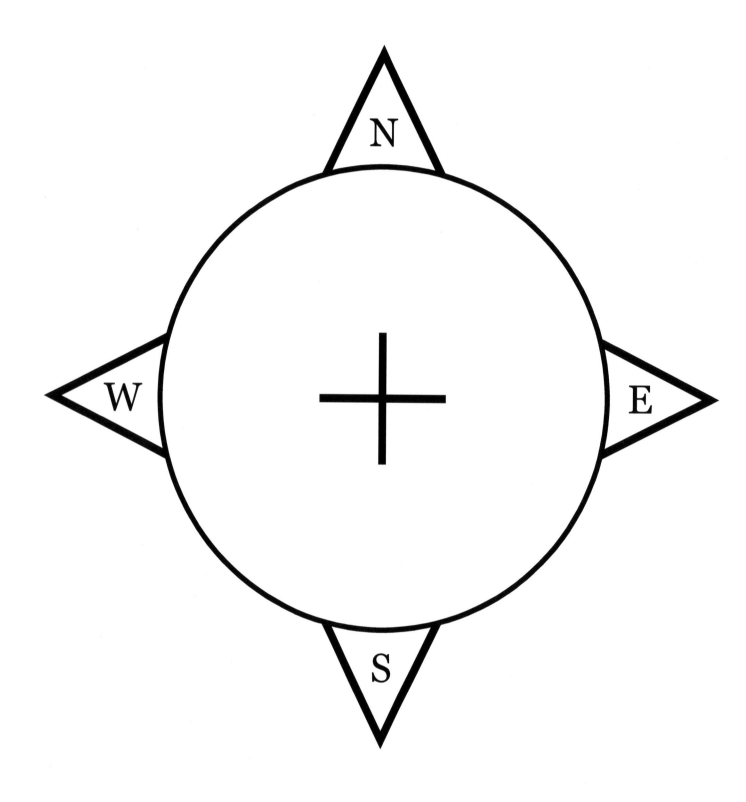

Template d.

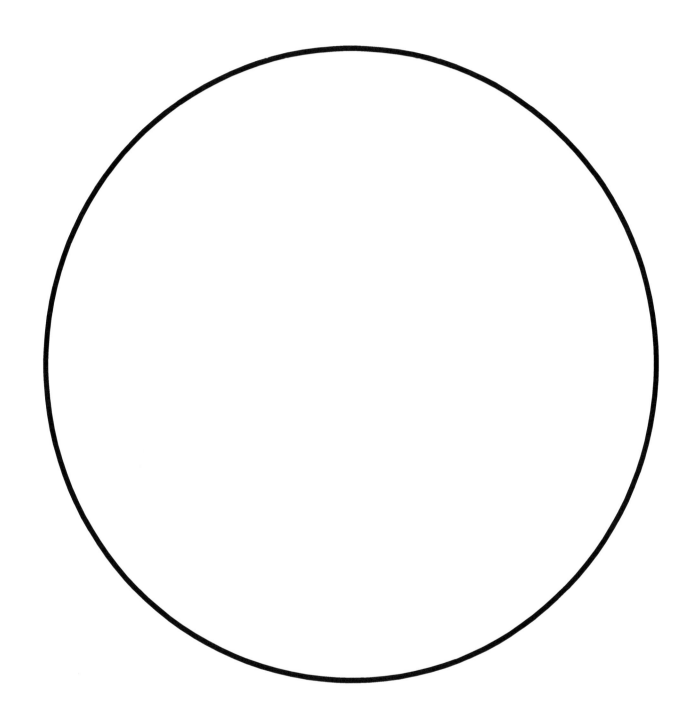

Template e.

Template f.

Lessons for Living Program

Name _____ Date _____

Section (Circle one):   Physical   Mental   Emotional   Spiritual

Lesson: _____

STUDENT NOTES

Name _____

Section _____ Lesson _____

SELF-INQUIRY PAGE

_____

_____

_____

_____

_____

_____

_____

_____

_____

_____

_____

_____

_____

_____

_____

_____

_____

_____

_____

_____

_____

_____

_____

_____

Name _____

Section _____ Lesson _____

<u>MY KNOWLEDGE PAGE</u>
(INFORMATION, DISCOVERIES, AND QUESTIONS)

_____

_____

_____

_____

_____

_____

_____

_____

_____

_____

_____

_____

_____

_____

_____

_____

_____

_____

_____

_____

_____

_____

Name _____

Section _____ Lesson _____

<u>NOTES TO MYSELF</u>

_____

_____

_____

_____

_____

_____

_____

_____

_____

_____

_____

_____

_____

_____

_____

_____

_____

_____

_____

_____

_____

Certificate of Participation

_____

Name

Lessons for Living Program™

_____

Location

_____

Date

Facilitator

Congratulations!

Group Warm-up Ideas

1. *Introductions*–Interview another student to obtain information: siblings, pets, favorite—music, color, sport, etc. Take turns introducing each other to the group.

2. *Personal Symbol*–Draw a symbol for yourself as a flower, building, automobile, musical instrument . . . Share with the group.

3. *My Favorite Things*–Write down some of your favorite things on a "pizza wedge" shape that has been cut from a large paper circle. Share your favorites with the group.

4. *Just Like Me*–One student stands in the center of a circle and asks the group: "Who likes _____ just like me?" Students who like what is named must rise and find a different chair along with the center person. The student who is left without a seat goes to the center for a turn.

5. *Tropical Island*–You are going to a tropical island where you will have a place to sleep, food to eat, and clothing to wear. You can only take one object with you. Share with the group what that would be and why.

6. *Life Story*–Tell your life story to the group in three minutes. Use a timer.

7. *Elephant, Rabbit, Palm Tree*–A student stands in the center of a group circle. They point to someone and say "elephant," "rabbit," or "palm tree." The person who was selected must quickly be the middle section of what is named; students on their left and right complete the formation. Whoever is incorrect is "out." For elephant—the middle person bends over and puts arms together to form a trunk; the left and right students hold their arms down like large ears. For rabbit—the middle person wiggles their nose and holds arms up as ears; the left and right students thump their outside foot. For palm tree—the middle person stands straight with arms at side; the left and right students raise and wave their arms like fronds.

8. *Clues*–On an index card, write clues about yourself. Facilitator collects cards to read the clues out loud. Students guess the identity.

9. *Free Movement*–Play some upbeat music and move freely around the room. Incorporate scarves, "dress-up" clothes, and/or percussion instruments.

10. *Good News*–Make up a headline for something good that happened to you last week.

The Emergence of
A New Educational Paradigm in America

Our educational system plays a major role in rebirthing our society to where the primary focus is on learning how to live rather than how to make a living. A good education encourages the integrated individual to discover his vocation, responsibilities, and creative nature, or as Socrates said, "know thyself."

A holistic perspective is the appropriate trajectory for our school communities. This education emphasizes the connection of all life and respects the learning that takes place not only through the mind, but also through the body, feelings, and imagination. Holistic education respects the autonomy of students and supports our children in developing their innate potentialities that can contribute positively to society. It guides them in making wise choices for creating their lives, choices that in turn affect us all.

Seeds have been strewn along the nation's path for over two hundred years in hope that a new dominant worldview would take hold. Notable historical figures (theorists, philosophers, educators, psychologists, and radicals) courageously voiced their opposition to a social structure heavily fertilized by state-serving values. Western culture continually propagated a crop of dutiful citizens ready to garnish a land of materialism. It was this predominant worldview—like weeds that become pervasive and familiar—that prevented any "holistic" pedagogy in education to fully take root and flourish.

In the early days of America we can see how schooling began—narrowly focused to the "needs" of the time. European influences helped establish ideas for instilling Protestant moral values to students. Early classrooms were preoccupied with discipline and order, and active learning was deemed less important. An American standard textbook, *The New England Primer*, was introduced in 1690 to teach reading and religion, and it was used until the beginning of the nineteenth century. As divisive class structures grew, children of wealthy families often continued on to secondary schools to pursue professions in law, medicine, or the ministry. Poor children received no formal schooling and learned mostly through apprenticeship. Preparation for an efficient working class suitable for industry was taking shape.

Humanistic ideas during Italy's Renaissance period in the fourteenth century, which then spread to Northern Europe into the sixteenth century, would later inspire new thinkers in the United States. Influenced by ideals expressed in the literature of ancient Greece, many humanists sought to develop an educational philosophy that was well rounded and unfolded an individual's talents in all intellectual and physical areas rather than specialization in a specific discipline. In 1423, Vittorino da Feltre (1378–1446) an Italian humanist, began a school known as *Casa Gicosa*, "Merry House." Students from diverse backgrounds and ages came to study there in a cheerful environment. A range of humanistic subjects was taught: the arts, Latin, Greek and Roman literature, religion, mathematics, history, and physical development.

John Amos Comenius (1592–1670) a seventeenth-century visionary who lived and worked throughout Europe, has been called the "Father of Modern Education." He was a forerunner to future holistic education pioneers, Rousseau and Pestalozzi of the eighteenth century, and believed in formulating education according to "nature," and relying more on the power of learning by observation. Comenius led a movement for "universal education," which advocated schooling for all children, including the impoverished and women. His pictorial children's textbook, *Orbis Pictus*, gained much popularity and was used for over two centuries. An English philosopher named John Locke (1632–1704) developed a theory that the mind was made up of faculties such as thinking, perceiving, discriminating, comparing, and recalling, These powers were best exercised so as to obtain knowledge by supplementing book learning with sensory impressions from natural objects.

Locke's work influenced the French educator, Jean-Jacques Rousseau (1710–1778), who would have a great effect on twentieth-century education in America. Rousseau believed that the aim of education should be on the natural development of the learner. He suggested that book learning not be introduced until a child was fifteen years of age, allowing for a primary focus during childhood to be on cultivating the body and its senses. Learning by experience, and encouraging a child's "true gifts of nature" were some of the important early "holistic" education principles that he proposed.

Enlightenment ideas filtered into attitudes concerning education in eighteenth-century America, and with that colonists decided that more practical content be added to the school curriculum. The advent of commercialism and secularism in the Western world also urged education to address the needs of everyday life. In 1751, Benjamin Franklin (1706–1790) helped form an academy that offered courses in history, geography, modern language, geometry, and astronomy—which provided training for enterprise and personal advancement. His revolutionary ideas, however, would not easily replace mainstream attitudes for the "homogenization" of individuals by the invested authority of school "masters" and directed allegiance to state leaders.

At the beginning of the early 1800s in Europe, international attention was given to the first important educator to apply the "holistic" ideas of Rousseau. Johann Pestalozzi (1746–1827) of Switzerland established residential schools on working farms for orphans and paupers. He honored the natural development of each individual by encouraging learning from observation rather than the memorization of facts. Learning began with first-hand observation and moved gradually to the abstract realm of words and ideas. The teacher's job was to guide by selecting experiences that would direct the child to this end. Pestalozzi's motto for education: "Learning by head, hand, and heart." After working with Pestalozzi for two years, another revered European, German educator Fredrich Froebel (1782–1852), began his own schools in Central Europe. He became the founder of kindergarten or "children's garden," where children were nurtured to grow naturally like plants. The kindergarten provided a free environment with materials for self-activity that fostered playful spontaneity.

Another noteworthy inspiration for "holistic" philosophy was Russian-born Leo Tolstoy (1828–1910)—moral thinker, writer, and social reformer. Tolstoy created a school in the mid-1800s on his personal estate, where local peasant children came to learn through casual chats and lessons. His school of *Yasnaya Polana* was considered the first to use the theo-

ries of a democratic school, preceding A.S. Neill's progressive work in 1921.

In the 1830s in America, the New England Transcendentalists created the first holistic education movement. There were approximately fifteen leading figures in this group. Among them were William Ellery Channing, Ralph Waldo Emerson, George Ripley, Henry David Thoreau, and Bronson Alcott. The importance of individuality and spiritual development was the central impetus of the Transcendentalists. They rejected moral disciplines imposed by American culture, and were in opposition to many social institutions. The Transcendentalists were advocates for an educational philosophy that respected the natural growth of every child's interests, abilities, and which allowed an exploration of nature's lessons firsthand.

William Ellery Channing (1780–1842) and Ralph Waldo Emerson (1803–1882) were great thinkers of the Transcendentalist movement. Both men were Unitarian ministers who steadfastly preached about recognizing the spiritual identity of man's nature. Channing spoke of his belief that within every person is a potential for spiritual realization, and education must strive to unfold one's individual faculties and powers. He criticized the narrow striving for material status of American culture, and Channing voiced his objections to the themes of nationalism and of the conservative limits on democracy. Emerson's teachings expressed how a child's life is "chosen and foreordained," whereby an educator's task is to provide the necessary conditions for this unique unfolding.

George Ripley (1802–1880) was the head teacher of the Brook Farm School; a communal environment that centered on agriculture and education. The school fostered responsibility, personal involvement, and a close relationship between children and adults. Henry David Thoreau (1817–1862) was a Unitarian minister and a Transcendentalist educator who taught in Concord, Massachusetts for a number of years before retreating to Walden Pond. He professed that education should help to develop a person's "genius" or creative potential, and "learning by doing" was a most effective teaching method.

Bronson Alcott (1799–1888), who was the most radical of the educators, worked fervently to promote spiritual freedom in education. His ideas much aligned with Pestalozzi, led him to open the Temple School in 1834. Situated in a Masonic temple, Alcott created a comfortable atmosphere where students could explore real objects. Self-expression, imagination, and a personal responsibility for order were encouraged. The school was forced to close after four years by opponents to Alcott's convictions and political viewpoints that threatened conservative Protestant pedagogy.

The move toward state-supported non-secular schools for children in the United States began with common (elementary) schools during the 1820s. Momentum was gained in 1837 when Horace Mann (1796–1859), a Massachusetts lawyer and politician, was appointed the position of secretary for the nation's first state Board of Education. His most famous reform was the establishment of the first public normal (teacher training) school in Massachusetts, an example that other states later followed.

An educational ladder was now developing in America. The common school that had focused on basic studies, which originally consisted of one teacher and pupils ranging in age from six to thirteen, expanded their curriculum to include science, nature study, spelling, and history. After completion of elementary school, middle-class students could continue to study at a vocational or technical school. An upper-class child, who was sometimes privately tutored, could enter secondary school or Latin grammar school to prepare for entrance to a university.

A new society was forming in the United States by the mid-nineteenth century, complicated by discoveries in physical and biological sciences. Industrialism and capitalism began to take hold, pushing for minds to be "trained" for newer kinds of instruction. By 1861, secondary schools offered a wealth of subjects for students to study, emphasizing science. The common school curriculum, which concentrated on material from texts—arithmetic, history, geography, the *Noah Webster American Spelling Book*, and *McGuffey's Eclectic Readers*—expanded to include courses in

368

science and nature.

The Industrial Revolution anchored public education in the United States. By the 1870s, tax-supported public school systems were established and compulsory attendance laws appeared. By the 1880s, several million immigrants were absorbed into America, resulting in the institution of public education to instill factory work habits of punctuality, discipline, and obedience. Larger schools replaced common elementary schools with student population divided by age; seating was arranged in formal rows for teaching efficiency.

New methods of instruction, formulated by the theories of German psychologist Johann Fredrich Herbart (1776–1841) were reinforced. Herbart proposed that subject matter be presented in a systematic sequence and imparted to students by well-trained teachers who used psychological insight to gain interest. His theories reflected a teacher-curriculum focus using lesson plans, drills, memorization, and a rigid daily timetable. As Herbart's remedy to educate large numbers of children and have them acquire a great deal of information within a short time gained support, interest in Pestalozzi's child-centered approach diminished.

Francis Parker (1837–1902) was a public school holistic educator in Massachusetts. He was able to have widespread influence on American educators through public lectures and through his position as the Superintendent of Schools in Quincy, Massachusetts. His book, *Talks on Pedagogics*, (1894) argues against traditional teaching methods that favored the teacher as authoritarian and the student passive. He proposed that all aspects of humanness be recognized and developed, believing that human nature was essentially good and aspired to the transcendent. Although respected, his education ideas remained on the quiet perimeter of mainstream society.

John Dewey (1859–1952), a major contributor of educational ideas, viewed education as serving a social agenda and called for a liberal progressive approach to educate the whole child. Subject matter must be actively engaging, evoke inquiry, and appeal to the child's present experience. Dewey believed that a culture's allegiance to traditional systems would eventually become futile, as the times demand change. The ideals of Francisco Ferrer (1859–1909) initiated a "Modern School" movement in Spain from 1901 to 1906. Followers in the United States established the Ferrer School in New York and later in New Jersey that thrived until the 1950s. Similar to the mindset of Rousseau, Tolstoy, and several French and Spanish anarchist educators, Ferrer advocated a transformation of the human worldview.

In the early twentieth century, two major pioneers in holistic education stimulated the European and American scene. Maria Montessori (1870–1952), an Italian physician turned educator, stunned the world with teaching techniques that successfully helped mentally challenged children progress in learning at the *Casa dei Bambini*, "Children's House," in Rome. It was here that she developed self-correcting sensorial materials that supported a child's cognitive growth. She initiated an important principle: Independent freedom for the child through self-activity in a "prepared environment," where the teacher acts as a guide. Her method is based on a concern for the physical, mental, and emotional growth of a child, while still retaining faith in the spiritual force that directs human development.

Rudolf Steiner (1861–1925), a prolific writer and mystical thinker, began his own Anthroposophy movement in 1900. In 1919, at the Waldorf-Astoria cigarette factory in Switzerland, Steiner was invited to teach the children of employees. That was where he started the popular Waldorf School. He believed, like Montessori, that human development naturally unfolded from a succession of stages, though Steiner focused more on the manifestation of the inner spiritual being than cognitive growth. He saw human nature as composed of a body, soul, and spirit—each level independent but connected. The Waldorf method is rooted in a spiritual framework that nurtures artistic expression to reveal one's true nature.

The educational frontier expanded rapidly in the United States during the twentieth century. Beginning in the 1920s, public education was influenced significantly on a national level by the interest of corporations, foundations, textbook publishers, teacher training institutions, teacher unions, and the government. By the 1950s, the military establishment worked to influence America's youth, and great efforts were made to train students in science to compete with a worldwide race for technological advancement. Another educator attempted to implant alternative philosophies of education in the mid-twentieth century in America. A.S. Neill (1883–1973), probably the most famous proponent of holistic education during his time, founded the Summerhill School in England. His school became the inspiration for the Free School movement in America during the 1960s and 1970s. This movement rejected common public school principles such as grading, frequent tests, and the unwavering power of teachers.

During the 1960s, serious social unrest and advancements in technology resulted in education becoming a focal point for cultural conflict. A group of radical thinkers who brought their attention to critiquing public schools included John Holt, George Dennison, and Herbert Kohl. They argued that public education did not serve the needs of a student's normal growth. They voiced their criticism of predigested textbooks, grades, tests, competitive striving, and a focus of study not relevant to real life issues. The rebelliousness generated by youth in the 1960s was directly related to society's preoccupation with yielding the human spirit to conformity, authority, and indoctrination of patriotism.

The American Montessori Association was established in 1960, offering an alternative accreditation and teacher training. Public interest increased, which brought Montessori schools around the globe. Steiner's Waldorf schools also expanded, reaching over forty countries by the new century. These private schools both became beacons, attracting a population of society disillusioned with traditional education. In the 1970s, critics of public education in America caused some holistic changes to manifest with the trial of "open classrooms," and the introduction of magnet schools that encouraged racial integration.

Alternative schools were developed in the 1980s, which helped to keep "failing" students within the system by providing vocational skills, but little attention was given to these students' emotional needs that crippled the learning process. In 1991, the first charter school—free from state laws and district regulations but within the framework of public education, opened in Minnesota. By the year 2000, thirty-seven states had established this option from conventional education, with many charter schools establishing positive learner-based principles into their curriculum.

During the twentieth century, three psychologists, Carl Jung, Abraham Maslow, and Carl Rogers, each brought forth significant concepts on human development that interfaced with an emerging holistic framework. Other notables such as Margaret Naumberg, Jonathan Kozol, Kieran Egan, Paul Goodman, John Taylor Gatto, Joseph Chilton Pearce, John Miller, Paulo Freire, and Ron Miller have contributed ideas and support for an education based on equality, truth, and connection.

J. Krishnamurti (1895–1986), a spiritual teacher, articulated ideas on the holistic theme of peace and education. His numerous literary works are filled with spiritual wisdom concerning man and his relationships. His book, *Education and the Significance of Life* (1953), remains a classic in the study of holistic education. James Moffet (1929–1996) noted teacher and thinker wrote an inspiring book titled, *The Universal Schoolhouse* (1994), in which he envisioned the formation of de-centralized community learning networks that promote academic excellence, and address the personal development of learners of all ages. Parker Palmer (1939–), an educator and writer, has taken an activist stance toward revitalizing public education by renewal of the teacher's spirit. *The Courage To Teach* (1998) is a sequel to the important work *To Know As We Are Known* (1993) that offers a model for teaching authentically from a place of wholeness.

The twenty-first century holds a promise for education in America and around the world as its foundation of yesteryear crumbles along with many outdated cultural paradigms. I believe, along with others, that a true paradigm shift was energized amidst the turbulent 1960s. In the 1970s, the term "holism" was born to describe an emerging perspective in education that would meet the needs of generations to come. As we move forward, our nation reaches to embrace a spiritual worldview that is globally unifying and prioritizes reverence for the planet's ecosystem that we are all part of.

In America, productivity, competitiveness, and higher national standards linked to the interests of business will no longer be allowed to define public education. A new era is emerging where education policy transforms to meet its true goal: to awaken human potential for self-actualization. Holistic principles once portrayed as countercultural ease their way into mainstream public education, as some Montessori and Waldorf philosophies form in charter schools. Whole-child education, learner-based education, Quaker, homeschooling, community, cooperative, Democratic, Independent, Reggio Emilia-inspired education, and more movements, are gaining attention and momentum—each contain ideas that can contribute to a new model for public education.

Current voices, such as those of Alfie Kohn, Kenneth Robinson, Lynn Stoddard, and Diane Ravitch, have become louder as their messages for improving education for all children are being heard across the Internet. Seeds for a holistic approach to education are blowing swiftly about our precious earth. There is space now for them to freely grow and blossom as we boldly align to a peaceful, loving, and cooperative vision for society. A new educational paradigm that is taking root will enrich our children into the art of life, bringing personal fulfillment and uplifting the whole of humanity.

The holistic paradigm dissolves the traditional dichotomies between mind and body, between spirit and matter. The central tenet of the holistic worldview—and this is the basis for the term holistic—is its emphasis on the integration of the inner qualities of human life with the outer physical, social world. The holistic paradigm opposes the overly materialistic, rational, technocratic, and hierarchical tendencies of the industrial age in order to achieve a greater balance between individuality and community, creativity and tradition, intuition and reason, inner peace and objective success.
  — Ron Miller,
  What Are Schools For? Holistic Education in American Culture

Suggested Readings on Holistic Education Philosophy

Visit the A.E.R.O. (Alternative Education Resource Organization) website for additional references: www.educationrevolution.org

Voices of Pioneers

Alcott, A. Bronson (1938). *The Journals of Bronson Alcott.* (Odel Shepard, Ed.) Boston: Little Brown.

Dewey, John (1938). *Experience and Education.* New York: Macmillan.

Emerson, Ralph Waldo (1966). *Emerson on Education.* New York: Teachers College Press, Columbia University.

Froebel, Friedrich (1893). *The Education of Man* (1826;W. N. Hailmann, Trans.). New York: Appleton and Company.

Holt, John (1964). *How Children Learn.* New York: Pitman Publishing Company.

Jung, C. G. (1954). *Child Development and Education* (R.F.C. Hull, Trans.). In H. Read & M. Fordham & G. Adler (Eds.), The Development of Personality (2nd ed., Vol. 17), London: Routledge & Kegan.

Kohl, Herbert (1967). *36 Children.* New York: Penguin Group.

Krishnumurti, J. (1953, 1990). *Education and the Significance of Life.* London: Gollancz Ltd.

Maslow, A. (1975). *Some Educational Implications of the Humanistic Psychologies.* In T.B. Roberts (Ed.), Four Psychologies Applied to Education: Freudian, Behavioral, Humanistic, Transpersonal. Cambridge, MA: Schenkman Publishing Company.

Montessori, Maria (1973). *The Absorbent Mind* (1949; Claude Claremont Trans.). Madras, India: Kalakshetra.

Naumburg, Margaret (1928). *The Child and the World.* New York: Harcourt/Brace.

Neill, A.S. (1960). *Summerhill: A Radical Approach to Child Rearing.* Great Britain: Penguin Books.

Parker, Francis W. (1894). *Talks on Pedagogies*. New York: Kellogg.

Pearce, Joseph Chilton (1977). *Magical Child*. New York: Penguin Group.

Pestalozzi, J.H. (1907). *How Gertrude Teaches Her Children* (L.E.H. & F.C. Turner Trans.) (4rth ed.). London: Swan, Sonnenshein & Company.

Rogers, Carl (1969). *Freedom to Learn: A View of What Education Might Become*. Columbus, Ohio: Charles Merrill.

Rousseau, J.J. (1979). *Emile* (1762) (A. Bloom, Trans.). London: Penguin Books.

Steiner, Rudolph (1969). *Education as a Social Problem*. Spring Valley, NY: Anthroposophic Press.

Contemporary Voices

Eisler, Riane (2000). *Tomorrow's Children: A Blueprint for Partnership Education in the Twenty-First Century*. Boulder, CO: Westview Press.

Forbes, S. (2003). *Holistic Education: An Analysis of Its Ideas and Nature*. Brandon, VT: Foundation for Educational Renewal Box 328.

Gardner, Howard (2000). *Intelligence Reframed: Multiple Intelligences for the 21st Century*. New York: Basic Books.

Glazer, Steven (Ed), (1999). *The Heart of Learning: Spirituality in Education*. New York: Tarcher/Putnam.

Harrison, Steven (2001). *The Happy Child: Changing the Heart of Education*. Boulder, CO: Sentient Publications.

Kessler, Rachael (2000). *The Soul of Education: Helping Students Find Connection, Compassion and Character at School*. Alexandria, VA: ASCD.

Kohn, Alfie (1999). *The Schools Our Children Deserve: Moving Beyond Traditional Classrooms and "Tougher Standards."* Boston: Houghton Mifflin.

Kozol, Jonathan (1995). *Amazing Grace: The Lives of Children and the Conscience of a Nation*. New York: Crown Publishing.

Miller, John P. (1996). *The Holistic Curriculum*. Toronto: OISE Press.

Miller, Ron (1997). *What Are Schools For? Holistic Education in American Culture*. Brandon, VT: Holistic Education Press.

Moffett, James (1994). *The Universal Schoolhouse: Spiritual Awakening Through Education*. San Francisco: Jossey-Bass.

Orr, David (1992). *Ecological Literacy: Education and the Transition to a Postmodern World*. Albany, NY: SUNY Press.

Palmer, Parker J. (1993). *To Know As We Are Known: Education As A Spiritual Journey*. San Francisco: Harper.

Ravitch, Diane (2013). R*eign of Error: The Hoax of the Privatization Movement and the Danger to America's Public School*s. New York: Alfred A. Knoph.

Robinson, Ken (2001, 2011). *Out of Our Minds: Learning to be Creative*. United Kingdom: Capstone Publishing.

Seldin, Tim & Epstein, Paul (2003). The *Montessori Way: An Education for Life*. New York: DK Publishing.

Stoddard, Lynn (2010). *Educating for Human Greatness: An Expanded Second Edition*. Sarasota, Florida: Peppertree Press.

Uhl, Christopher (2011). *Teaching as if Life Matters: The Promise of a New Education Culture*. Baltimore, Maryland: John Hopkins University Press.

Select Books by Key Authors Who Have Influenced This Project

Atkins, Sally (2007). *The Expressive Arts Therapy Sourcebook*. North Carolina: John F. Blair Publisher.

Capachionne, Lucia (1991). *Recovery of Your Inner Child: The Highly Acclaimed Method for Liberating Your Inner Self*. New York: Simon & Schuster.

Cornell, Judith (1994). *Mandala: Luminous Symbols for Healing*. Illinois: Quest Books.

London, Peter (1989). *No More Secondhand Art: Awakening The Artist Within*. Massachusetts: Shambhala Publications, Inc.

McNiff, Shaun (1992). *Art As Medicine: Creating a Therapy of the Imagination.* Massachusetts: Shambhala Publications, Inc.

McNiff, Shaun (1998). *Trust The Process.* Massachusetts: Shambhala Publications, Inc.

Myss, Carolyn (1996). *Anatomy of the Spirit: The Seven Stages of Power and Healing.* New York: Crown Publishers, Inc.

Myss, Carolyn (1997). *Why People Don't Heal and How They Can.* New York: Three Rivers Press.

McFarland, Sonnie (2004). *Honoring the Light of the Child: Activities to Nurture Peaceful Living Skills in Young Children.* Colorado: Shining Mountains Press.

Rogers, Natalie (2009). *The Creative Connection: Expressive Arts as Healing.* California: Science & Behavior Books, Inc.

Rogers, Natalie (2011). *The Creative Connection for Groups: Person-Centered Expressive Arts for Healing and Social Change.* California: Science & Behavior Books, Inc.

About the Author

Lissa Masters, Ph.D., ATR, a registered art therapist, also holds several training certificates in expressive arts therapy and an advanced degree in holistic counseling. Her experience as an art educator spans over twenty years in both public and private schools working with children of all age levels. She is dedicated to helping improve the quality of education around the globe, and to ensure that a child's natural rights for education are upheld. Ms. Masters is also an ordained minister, and artist of diverse interests. Originally from the East Coast, she now resides in Sonoma County, California.

For further information, trainings, workshops, etc. —
www.lissamasters.com

Amazing Grace

Amazing Grace, how sweet the sound,
*That loves this soul as me.
I once was lost but now I'm found,
Was blind, but now I see.

'Twas Grace that taught my heart to fear.
And Grace, my fears relieved.
How precious did that Grace appear
The hour I first believed.

Through many dangers, toils and snares
I have already come;
'Tis Grace that brought me safe thus far,
and Grace will lead me home.

The Lord has promised good to me.
His word my hope secures.
He will my shield and portion be,
As long as life endures.

Yea, when this flesh and heart shall fail,
And mortal life shall cease,
I shall possess within the veil,
A life of joy and peace.

When we've been here ten thousand years
Bright shining as the sun,
We've no less days to sing God's praise
Then when we've first begun.

Amazing Grace, how sweet the sound,
*That loves all souls as me.
*We all were lost but now we are found,
*We were blind, but now we can see!

*Original lyrics by John Newton (1725—1807);
words modified by Lissa Masters 2016